THE HEALTHY
HORSE

THE HEALTHY
HORSE

CARING FOR YOUR HORSE – IN SICKNESS AND IN HEALTH

JANET L. ELEY
BVSc MRCVS

SWAN·HILL
PRESS

Title page photograph: C. L. Hocking

Copyright © 2000 Janet L. Eley

First published in the UK in 2000
by Swan Hill Press, an imprint of Airlife Publishing Ltd

British Library Cataloguing-in-Publication Data
A catalogue record for this book
is available from the British Library

ISBN 1 85310 964 9

Typeset by Servis Filmsetting Ltd.
Printed in Italy.

Swan Hill Press
an imprint of Airlife Publishing Ltd
101 Longden Road, Shrewsbury, SY3 9EB, England
E-mail: airlife@airlifebooks.com
Website: www.airlifebooks.com

DEDICATION

To my Mother

ACKNOWLEDGEMENTS

Thanks go to Gillian Jenkinson for all the illustrations.

I would like to thank:
The Blue Cross; Robert Eustace FRCVS, Chris Hocking and Phil Russell of Smith and Nephew for use of their photographs as credited.

Gary Khahkian M/Eq.D for providing the dental numbering chart on page 25 and for his expert dental work.

John Preece RSS., Steve Aldford and all the farriers who have allowed me to photograph their work.

John Brentnall BVSc, MRCVS and William Rosie BVM&S, MRCVS for allowing me to photograph them at work.

All the friends and clients who assisted by handling and providing horses for photography, especially; Vivienne Davies, Mynderley Stables; Petra Archer, Redwood Stables; The Wyke, Deb Dudley, Stuart Deane, Thomas Hollinshead, James Stimpson, Don Pearce, Hilary Holmes, Joy Humphreys, Sandra Hughes, Linda Morris, Oonagh O'Neil, Joan Rogers and Kelly Williams.

CONTENTS

PART ONE

KEEPING YOUR HORSE HEALTHY

It is necessary to recognise the signs of good health in order to detect the first signs of illness. Every horse is an individual so it is important to make a record of each animal's basic details. These can include normal temperature, pulse and respiratory rate, any existing scars or blemishes, feeding and exercise details, preventive medicine programmes and any known health problems. A horse in good health should be alert and interested in its immediate surroundings. It should have a shiny coat free from sores, and the skin should be supple and move freely over the underlying tissues. The eyes are normally bright and free from discharges or swelling of the lids, the nostrils also should be clean and the breathing regular, slow and quiet. The breath should not smell offensive. A healthy animal does not normally cough or have enlarged glands below the ears.

It is not healthy to be over or underweight. It is advisable to monitor the body condition regularly. The amount of faeces and urine

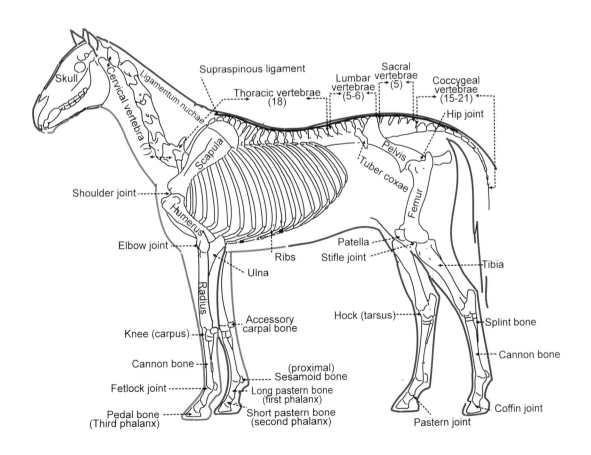

Fig.1. The skeleton of the horse.

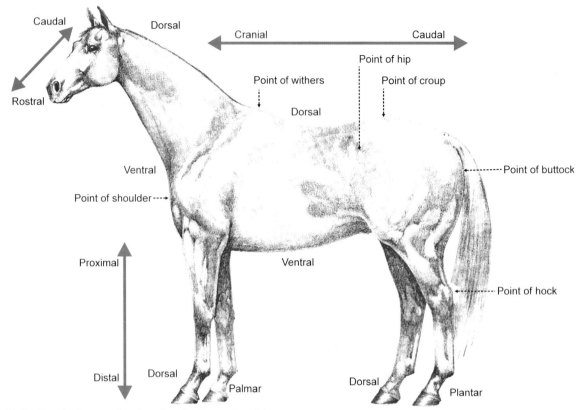

Fig.2a. Terminology used to describe direction and position.

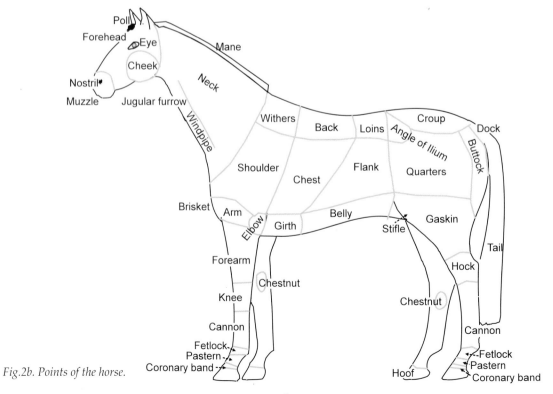

Fig.2b. Points of the horse.

passed obviously depends on the type and amount of feed given. A horse on a set feeding regime can be expected to pass similar amounts each day so it is easy to detect any differences which may be the early signs of disease. The horse should have a good appetite, be interested in its food and show no difficulty in chewing or swallowing. The horse should stand square and hold its head in a normal position, and when moving all the steps should be regular in length. It should move willingly and freely. The wear on the horse's shoes should be even.

It is important to know your own animal's pattern of behaviour. Some horses usually lie down in the field and stable whereas others only get down to roll. Often the owner notices quite subtle changes in behaviour which may be the early signs of illness. This is the time to check the horse's T.P.R.

NORMAL VALUES for an adult horse at rest:

TEMPERATURE (T)	37–38°C (98.5–100.5°F)
PULSE RATE (P)	25–40 per minute
RESPIRATION RATE (R)	8–16 per minute
CAPILLARY REFILL	less than 2 seconds
SKIN PINCH	less than 1½ seconds

The normal T.P.R. values for foals, young animals and ponies are higher than the adult horse values and those for donkeys are in the lower range.

HEALTH CHECKLIST

* behaviour   * posture
* eyes   * appetite
* nostrils   * thirst
* coat   * faeces
* body condition * urine

ASSESSING BODY WEIGHT

There is a variety of methods available to calculate body weight if a weighbridge is not available. A weight tape measure designed for horses can be used (Spillers or Daltons).

When the height and condition score is known the weight can be read off a nomogram. (See opposite.)

Alternatively the following formula may be used:

$$\text{Weight (kg)} = \frac{\text{Length (cms)} \times \text{Girth (cms)}^2}{11877}$$

The length is measured from the point of the shoulder to the point of the buttock (Carroll and Huntington 1988).

There is another formula using heart girth squared multiplied by length from the point of the shoulder to the hip and divided by 8,717. The heart girth circumference of the horse is measured by passing a tape over the withers and behind the elbows. The measurement is taken as the horse breathes out. This heart girth circumference is a useful measurement to take at weekly or monthly intervals to detect weight loss or gain.

Condition scoring is a method used to assess the amount of body fat under the skin. The neck, the ribcage and back and the pelvis are examined visually and by palpation. The condition of the horse is then given a score from 0 to 5.

Condition scoring

0 = emaciated
1 = poor
2 = fair
3 = good
4 = fat
5 = very obese

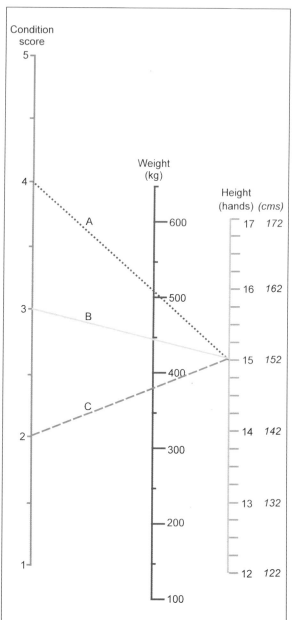

Fig.3. Weight nomogram e.g. Line C. 15 hh horse CS 2 weighs 380 kg. Line B CS 3 weighs 450 kg. Line A CS 4 weighs 500 kg.

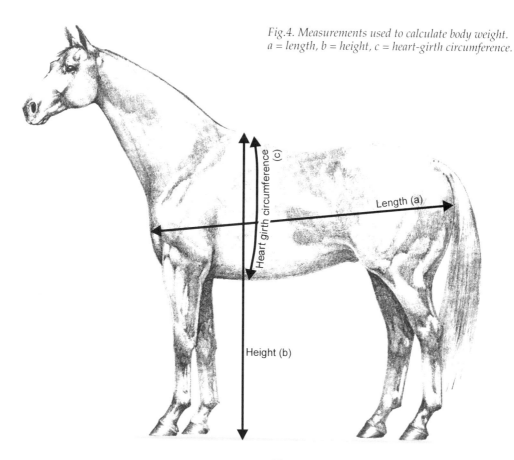

Fig.4. Measurements used to calculate body weight.
a = length, b = height, c = heart-girth circumference.

Neck

This is examined from the side to look at the general shape. Not all horses with a poor top line are thin, they may just lack muscle. It is best to feel just in front of the withers to get an idea of the firmness and width of the neck. Stallions tend to be cresty but are not necessarily fat. Fat horses will have folds of fat at the base of the neck and pads of fat in front of the shoulders.

Some animals with a poor conformation are ewe necked but not thin:

0 marked ewe neck; base of neck narrow/slack.
1 ewe neck; base of neck narrow/slack.
2 no top line; base of neck narrow/firm.
3 top line good but not cresty (NB stallions); base of neck firm.
4 crest starting fat folds; base wide/firm.
5 marked crest and fat folds; base very wide and firm.

Ribs and back

This area is examined from the side to see if the ribs and spine are visible. The mid ribcage is felt to assess the amount of fat covering the ribs. The vertebrae are well covered in the fat animal and it will have a table-top back. In obese cases a gutter runs along the backbone. It is not possible to feel the ribs even with firm pressure in very obese animals.

0 ribs and backbone easy to see and feel, skin drawn tightly over ribs, back bone sharp.
1 ribs and vertebrae well defined.
2 ribs just visible, backbone covered but easily felt.
3 ribs and vertebrae covered, ribs easily felt.
4 ribs felt only on firm pressure, gutter along backbone.
5 ribs buried in fat, table-top back with deep gutter.

CS = 3 (Condition score 3: good) (C. L. Hocking)

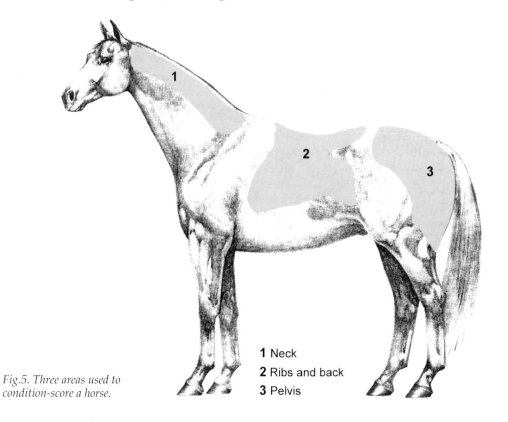

1 Neck
2 Ribs and back
3 Pelvis

Fig.5. Three areas used to condition-score a horse.

CS = 2 (Condition score 2: fair).

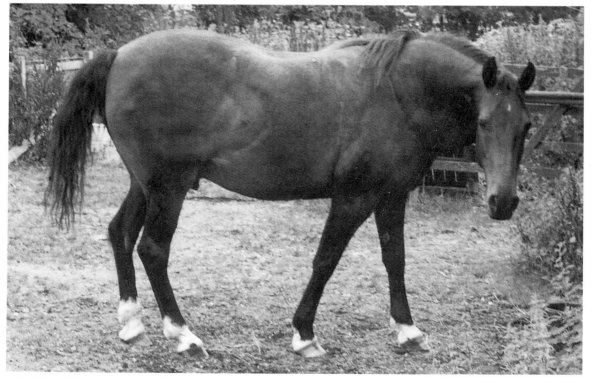

CS = 5 (Condition score 5: very obese).

Pelvis

The pelvis is best viewed from behind to assess the amount of flesh covering the bones. Thin animals will appear angular, with hollow flanks and a deep depression under the tail. The pelvis and croup will be easy to palpate. An obese horse will have a round rump, the inner thighs will touch and the gutter at the base of the tail will be deep. Remember that a hairy coat may be hiding a thin or fat animal so use your hands!

0 angular pelvis, hollow flanks, deep cavity under tail, skin tight.
1 pelvis/croup well defined, deep cavity under tail, skin supple.
2 rump flat, pelvis easily felt, cavity under tail.
3 pelvis covered, rump rounder, skin smooth.
4 pelvis well covered, only felt with firm pressure, gutter at root of tail.
5 pelvis buried in fat, deep gutter, skin distended.

To calculate the condition score, score each of the three sites separately. If the pelvis score differs from the neck or rib score by one point or more adjust it by 0.5 to give the correct score, e.g. neck score 3, rib and back 2, pelvis 3, actual score = 2.5.

In order to keep the horse in good health we usually have a health programme to include:

vaccinations
worming
external parasite control and skin care
routine dental checks
farriery and hoof care
correct nutrition
exercise

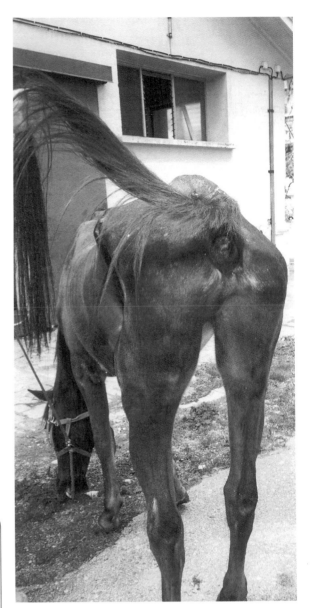

CS = 0 (Condition score 0: emaciated).

VACCINATIONS

It is important only to vaccinate animals which are in good health and are not stressed. They should not be travelled, competed or worked hard immediately before or after vaccination. Any animal which develops side effects or swelling at the vaccination site should be re-examined by the vet and the manufacturers of the vaccine informed. It is very uncommon to have a problem due to vaccination if the recommended procedure is followed.

Equines can be protected against tetanus, equine influenza virus and equine herpes virus 1 and 4.

It is sensible to vaccinate all horses. Tetanus is usually fatal in the horse and often animals which become infected with the influenza or herpes virus are ill for many months and are left with respiratory problems and poor performance when exercised. Tetanus vaccine is available as a combined vaccine with influenza or as a separate vaccine.

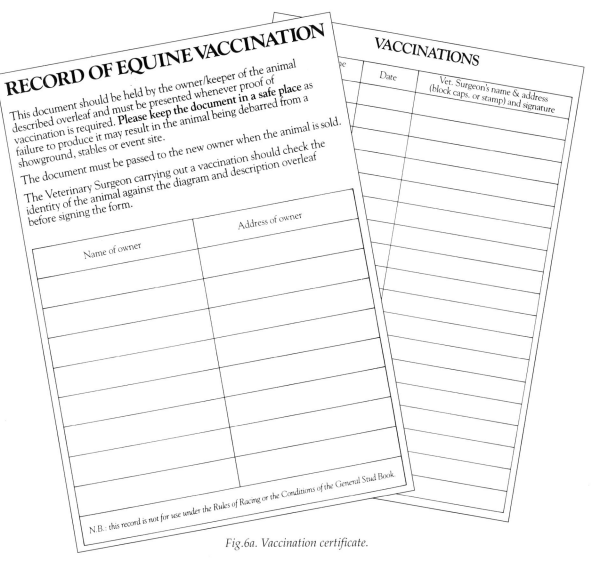

Fig.6a. Vaccination certificate.

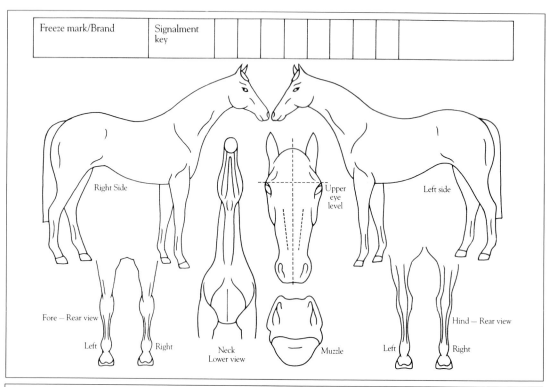

Freeze mark/Brand	Signalment key								

Right Side

Left side

Upper eye level

Fore — Rear view

Left Right

Neck
Lower view

Muzzle

Hind — Rear view

Left Right

Name of animal			No.	
Colour	Sex	Date of Birth		Approx. Adult Height
Head				
Neck				
LEGS	LF			
	RF			
	LH			
	RH			
Body			V.S. Stamp and signature:	
Place and Date				

Identification procedure: The above identification must be completed by a Veterinary Surgeon only.

The recommended procedure for identification is described in the F.E.I. booklet 'Identification of Horses'.

The diagram and written description must agree and must be sufficiently detailed to ensure the positive identification of the animal in future. White markings must be shown in red and the written description completed using **black ink in block capitals or typescript.** If there are no markings, this fact must be stated in the written description.

All head and neck whorls should be marked ("X") and described in detail. Other whorls should be similarly recorded in greys and in animals lacking sufficient other distinguishing marks. Acquired marks (" ") and other distinguishing marks, e.g. prophet's thumb mark ("△"), wall eye, etc., should always be noted.

Age: In the absence of documentary evidence of age, animals older than 8 years may be described as "aged".

Please leave blank: 'signalment key' top right hand box and 'No'.

Fig.6b. Vaccination certificate, reverse

Fig.7. Landmarks for intramuscular injection sites in the neck and rump.

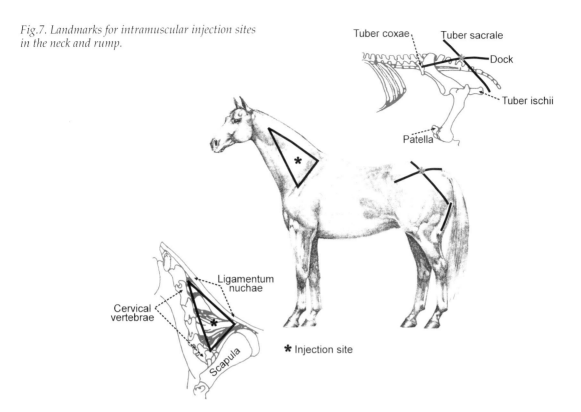

*Injection site

Intramuscular injection in the neck.

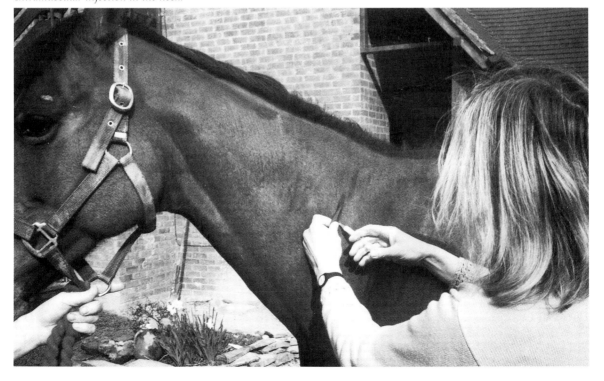

RECOMMENDED VACCINATION PROGRAMME		
Vaccine	Trade name	Primary course
Tetanus	Duvaxyn T Equip T Tetanus Toxoid	2 doses 4–6 weeks apart Booster after one year and then every 18–36 months
Equine Influenza strains A Equi/2 (Suffolk 89) A Equi/1 (Prague 56) A Equi/2 (Miami 63) A Equi/2 (Newmarket 2/93) A Equi/1 (Newmarket 77) A Equi/2 (Brentwood 79) A Equi/2 (Borlange 91)	Duvaxyn IE Plus and Prevac Pro EQUIP F	Primary course 2 doses 4–6 weeks apart 1st and 2nd booster at 6 month intervals then yearly Primary course 2 doses 6 weeks apart 1st booster 5 months after 2nd dose. Next boosters at 12 to 15 month intervals
Equine Herpes virus EVH-1 and EVH-4 EVH-1	DUVAXYN EHV 1, 4 Pneumabort K	Primary course 2 doses 4–6 weeks apart. Booster every 6 months
Equine Viral Arteritis (EVA)	Artervac	Primary course 2 doses 4 weeks apart and completed at least 3 weeks before the start of breeding. Annual boosters. This vaccine is used to protect stallions from infection and to prevent them becoming viral shedders and infecting the mares they serve at mating.

All vaccinations have a primary course followed by boosters. Some authorities, e.g. *Fédération Équestre Internationale* (FEI) and the Jockey Club require that booster vaccines are given at specific times in order for a horse to compete on their premises and under their rules. As an owner it is wise to check on these rules if there is any chance that you may wish to ride on a race-course.

Foals usually start their primary vaccination course at three to five months of age, when the passive immunity they received from their dam wanes. These maternal antibodies pass to the foal in the colostrum (first milk produced at foaling time). Pregnant mares are given boosters three to six weeks prior to foaling so that the foal will receive the maximum protection.

Vaccination certificates are signed by the vet and are proof that the animal is vaccinated. They have a diagram and written description of the animal. If you purchase a new horse it is wise to check that the vaccination certificate matches the horse! If no certificate is available presume the animal is not vaccinated. If you fail to have the required booster within twelve months of the last booster the horse will have to start the course again. It is best to keep a record of when the boosters are due so they are not forgotten. The manufacturers advise that vaccine boosters are given at set intervals so that the horse's immunity to that disease remains high, i.e. the horse is protected.

The success of vaccination depends not only on the correct administration of the vaccine but also on the health, nutritional status and age of the animal. Animals already on medication or with illnesses will not produce a good immunity to vaccines. Vaccines are used in disease control in combination with good animal husbandry and management.

WORMING

Internal parasites are present in all equines. They cause a variety of clinical diseases in their hosts depending on the species of worm and the numbers involved. The effect may be:

weight loss	emaciation
colic	diarrhoea
staring coat	tail rubbing
anaemia	jaundice
swollen legs	sheath swelling
debility	nasal discharge
coughing	poor performance
ill thrift	anorexia
bowel obstruction	death

Animals which are heavily infested are debilitated which makes them prone to other diseases.

As you can see from the table below, most of the adult worms are in the horse's gut where they damage the bowel wall. They shed eggs which pass out in the horse's faeces to contaminate the pasture. Infective larvae hatch out of the eggs and are then eaten by the grazing horse. The life-cycle of the parasite depends on the species. The worm larvae migrate through various tissues and organs causing damage before emerging as young adult worms in the gut lumen. The migration path and the time taken for the parasite to complete its life-cycle varies with the species. The stable and grassland management system has to be considered before a worming programme can be designed to suit the individual. Your vet is the best person to advise on worming as he knows your particular situation. All animals on the same premises which share the grazing must be treated as a herd. Fields which are overgrazed and overstocked and small turn-out paddocks will have more problems than those which are better managed. Pasture management methods which include removal of dung twice weekly, alternate grazing, destocking or resting fields will all reduce re infestation and therefore the number of treatments needed.

Harrowing should only be done in dry, hot weather when the parasites will be desiccated; at any other time it just spreads the larval worms all over the pasture.

Horses do not like to graze the areas they have dunged and so create roughs and lawns. If dung clearing is practised, more of the pasture can be grazed. Small paddocks can be cleared daily; larger areas at least twice a week during the grass growing season and once a week in frost and cold winter conditions. Pasture larval counts when considered with local temperature and rainfall will show the efficacy of the worming programme and warn of potential problems.

MAIN INTERNAL PARASITES OF THE HORSE		
Type	Species	Location of adult worm in host
Large redworm	Strongylus vulgaris	Caecum/Colon
	Strongylus edentatus	Caecum/Colon
Small redworm	Cyathostomes	Caecum/Colon
Roundworm	Parascaris equorum	Small intestine
Bots	Gastrophilus	Larvae in stomach (adult=fly)
Threadworm	Strongyloides westeri	Small intestine
Seat/Pinworm	Oxyuris equi	Colon/Rectum
Tapeworm	Anoplocephala perfoliata	Ileum/Caecum
Lungworm	Dictyocaulus arnfieldi	Lung/Bronchi

The drugs (anthelmintics) used to worm horses in the U.K., are in one of the following chemical groups:

1 Benzimidazole: Panacur, Telmin, Bayverm, Equivurm plus and Equitac
2 Ivermectin: Eqvalan, Panomec and Furexel
3 Pyrantel: Strongid P and Pyratape P
4 Moxidectin: Equest

These drugs kill the parasite in different ways:

Benzimidazoles interfere with the uptake of food by the worm.
Ivermectins cause a non-spastic paralysis of the worm.
Pyrantel causes a spastic paralysis.
Moxidectin causes paralysis

Some drugs have a specific action against certain worms and some kill the adult parasite in the gut lumen along with the immature migrating larvae.

The inter-dosing interval differs for each of the groups of drugs:

Drug	Dosing interval
Ivermectins	8–10 weeks
Benzimidazole	6–8 weeks
Pyrantel	4–6 weeks
Moxidectin	13 weeks

In order to use the correct drug at the correct dose rate it is necessary to have the following information:

1 The age and weight of the horse(s) to be treated
2 Is it pregnant?
3 Is it healthy?
4 Is it on medication?
5 Does it have worms?

By examining faeces samples at the laboratory using a variety of tests the number and types of worms present will be known. Blood tests can detect anaemia and raised beta globulins in gut damage due to strongyle infestation; there is also a blood test specifically for tapeworm infestation. Some horses appear healthy, but have a high worm burden and are contaminating the pasture with millions of eggs a day.

The faecal egg reduction test is used to test for drug resistant parasites. Faeces samples are taken seven to twenty-one days after worming, and the results compared with the pre-worming sample. This shows how effective the wormer has been. Small strongyles (cyathostomes) have become resistant to many of the drugs in the benzimidazole group at the normal dose rate. This has been caused by overuse of these drugs at incorrect dose rates and dosing intervals.

WORMING PROGRAMMES Spring and summer routine				
Year	APR	MAY	JUN	JUL	AUG
1	Ivermectin every 8–10 weeks				
2	Benzimidazoles every 6 weeks				
3	Pyrantel every 4 weeks				
4	Moxidectin every 13 weeks				

WINTER WORMING PROGRAMME		
Month	Parasite	Treatment
Sep	Tapeworm	Pyrantel (2 x dose)
Oct	nil	nil
Nov	Small redworm	Fenbendazole (5 day)
Dec	Bots	Ivermectin/Moxidectin
Jan	nil	nil
Feb	Small redworm	Fenbendazole (5 day)
Mar	Tapeworm	Pyrantel (2 x dose)

The conditions needed for grass to grow, warmth and moisture, are also ideal for worm larvae to hatch from the eggs passed out in the dung. At temperatures over 7°C the eggs hatch. The infective third stage larvae move out of the dung onto blades of grass where they can be eaten by any grazing animal. Most horses spend more time at grass from spring to autumn and ingest many larvae. It is necessary to worm regularly in the spring and summer.

Choose one of the drug groups and use that wormer at its correct dosing interval for the entire season. The next year a different drug is used, i.e. rotate the wormers on an annual basis during the spring to autumn grazing season. Between March and September most animals will be routinely wormed every four to thirteen weeks depending on the chemical used that particular year.

Horses which are grazed individually, or where pasture hygiene is rigidly practised may need fewer treatments, assessed by the results of faecal worm egg counts (WEC).

Selective dosing can be used all year round if monthly WECs are done on all the herd. Only those animals with a positive count need treatment.

If a new horse is introduced onto a system, it should be wormed with a five day course of Fenbendazole (Panacur equine guard) prior to going onto the pasture. This will prevent contamination of the grazing with new worm strains which may have anthelmintic resistance.

All horses should be wormed before moving onto new grazing. Elderly and debilitated animals should have a faecal WEC and the results discussed with your vet prior to any drugs being given.

Tapeworm

The mature tapeworm sheds segments full of eggs in the dung. The eggs are eaten by the forage mite (oribatid mite). The mite lives on grassland, hay and bedding. The cysticercoid stage larvae are eaten by the horse and take six to ten weeks to develop into egg laying adults. The adults attach by suckers to the gut wall at the ileocaecal junction (where the small intestine meets the caecum) and can cause impactions (blockages), ruptures and peritonitis. They are responsible for about 20% of surgical colics and also chronic recurrent colic (abdominal pain).

A blood test, the Elisa method IGGT test can detect animals with a large number of tapeworms. These animals are at great risk of developing gut damage.

Pyrantel at double the normal dose rate is the only drug available to treat tapeworm infestation in equines. As part of a worming programme it is used in March and September. Infestation is greatest in heathland areas and acid soils – a favoured environment for the intermediate host, the oribatid mite. Animals which are debilitated or have a history of laminitis should not be treated with pyrantel (double dose) unless they have a tapeworm burden and should be carefully monitored. It is recognised that some drugs can precipitate a laminitis attack in high risk animals.

Worming drugs

Bots

Horse bot flies (Gastrophilus intestinalis) lay eggs on the legs and abdomen of grazing horses in the summer. They are licked off by the horse and the larvae hatch and burrow to the stomach where they stay for about ten months before passing out in the dung. The adult fly emerges from the pupa to complete the life-cycle. Ivermectin or Moxidectin are used to treat bots in December after the frost has killed the flies and

Fig.8. Life-cycle of the tapeworm.

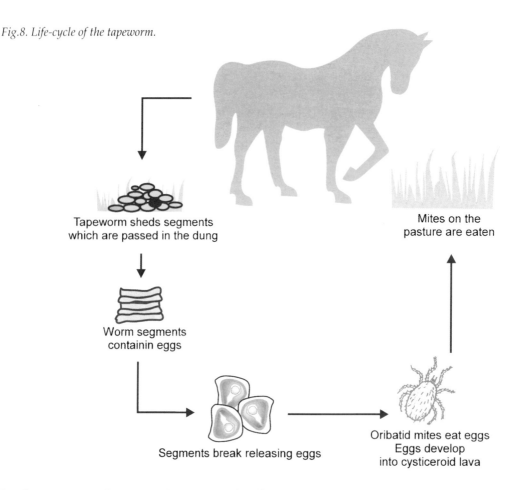

Tapeworm sheds segments
which are passed in the dung

Worm segments
containin eggs

Segments break releasing eggs

Oribatid mites eat eggs
Eggs develop
into cysticeroid lava

Mites on the
pasture are eaten

the bots are in the stomach. Insecticides/fly repellents applied to the horse in the summer will stop the flies laying eggs on the horse. The eggs can be removed from the horse's coat with Sellotape or special bot fly combs or knives.

Small redworm

This is the most important parasite because of its ability to delay development as larval cysts within the walls of the caecum and colon in the autumn. The larvae continue to develop in the spring when large numbers emerge from the gut. Both the encysted stage and the emerging larvae can cause serious disease, even death. Elderly animals and those under six months of age are particularly at risk, the highest risk occurring from late autumn to early spring. Animals

should be wormed in November and February with a five day course of fenbendazole to remove small redworm. Many small strongyle strains show resistance to other drugs in the benzimidazole group.

Large redworm

This used to be the most important parasite affecting the horse's gut. The larvae migrate through various tissues and some species damage the walls of arteries in the gut. This causes death to the part of the bowel supplied by the thrombosed vessel and acute colic. The incidence of this infection decreased when ivermectins became available in the U.K. as these are effective against both the larval and adult stages of large redworm.

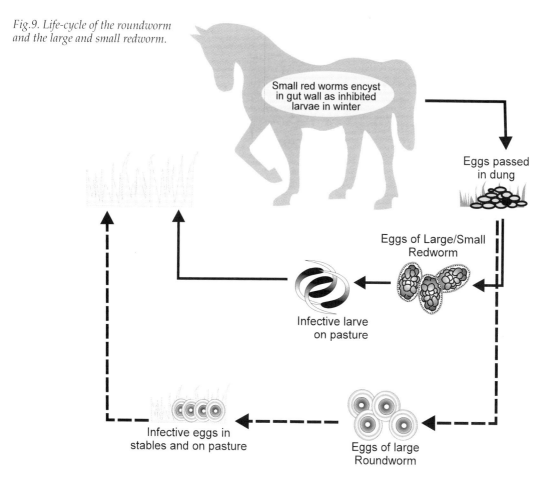

Fig.9. Life-cycle of the roundworm and the large and small redworm.

Small red worms encyst in gut wall as inhibited larvae in winter

Eggs passed in dung

Eggs of Large/Small Redworm

Infective larve on pasture

Infective eggs in stables and on pasture

Eggs of large Roundworm

Lungworm

Lungworms cause respiratory problems in adult horses and ponies, usually coughing and ill thrift. The infected larvae are passed out in the dung of affected donkeys and foals which may not show signs of the disease. The larvae are eaten by grazing horses and migrate through the bloodstream to the lungs. They rarely develop into egg-laying adults in the horse. In the donkey the larvae do mature to adults and eggs are coughed up, swallowed and pass out in the dung. Faeces can be used to test for lungworm in the foal and donkey but not in the horse, washings from the lungs of horses will detect the infection. Ivermectin is the drug of choice to treat lungworm infestation. It has become less common both in the donkey and horse over the last few years, but it is always wise to dose donkeys prior to moving them onto new pasture. Lungworms can survive for a long time on pasture and infect grazing animals for years to come.

Threadworm and roundworm

Threadworms live in the small intestines of young foals. They become infected soon after birth, either through the dam's milk or by the larvae penetrating the skin. Foals develop an immunity to this infection after six months of age. Heavy infestations cause diarrhoea, dullness and loss of appetite. Ivermectin is the drug of choice for threadworm, the alternative being fenbendazole at seven times the standard dose. Foals should be treated from four weeks old.

Roundworms are very large when mature and

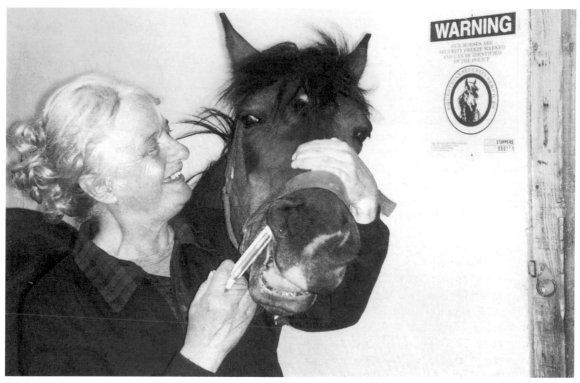

Dosing with a worming paste in a syringe

may cause blockages in the small intestine, failure to gain weight and emaciation. The female can lay millions of sticky, thick shelled eggs which can survive for years on stable walls and floors. These eggs containing infective larvae are picked up by the foal. The larvae migrate via the blood to the liver and lungs; this stage causes fever, coughing and anorexia. Yearlings develop an immunity at eighteen months old. Mares should be wormed prior to foaling, their udders washed to remove any eggs, and be provided with a clean pasture. Stables should be power cleaned and disinfected before being used as foaling boxes. All three groups of drugs are effective against ascarids.

Anthelmintics are available as pastes in dosing syringes and in feed additives as powder or liquid. Whichever preparation is used the animal must swallow the whole dose. If the drug is mixed in food you must watch while it is eaten and replace any spillages. All the products have full instructions for use and worming advice. It is advisable to wash your hands before and after handling medicines, and do not allow children to handle these products. Owners can always seek veterinary advice if they do not understand the instructions or there are any problems.

WORMING CHECKLIST

* follow the instructions on the product leaflet
* use the correct dose and dosing interval
* use a programme to suit your management system
* remove dung from the pasture 2 x week
* treat all the herd at the same time
* monitor results with WECs
* treat all foals and youngsters from 4 weeks old
* treat all newcomers before mixing with the herd
* treat all the herd before moving onto new pasture
* dispose of all packaging correctly
* do not treat sick or debilitated animals without seeking veterinary advice

SKIN CARE

The skin and coat need daily care and inspection. Grooming includes washing the dock region and the udder or sheath. Tack, rugs and grooming equipment must be correctly cleaned and maintained to prevent the spread of infection and injury. All tack and rugs must be properly fitted or the skin can be damaged, e.g. girth galls, saddle sores and biting injuries (at the corners of the mouth and the bars). Back muscles may also be damaged by poorly fitting saddles. Animals which gain or lose a lot of weight may need their saddles changed if they no longer fit correctly.

Grooming is the ideal time to check for any skin disorders and new injuries. It also means the horse is tied up and is being handled in a relaxed and calm way. Grooming should be a pleasant experience and a confidence builder for both horse and groom. There are many grooming aid products on the market, horse shampoos, sprays to make the coat shine, sheath cleaners etc. These are not really necessary when elbow grease and plain soap and water will normally do the job. There are a wide range of detergents for washing machines and many tack cleaning and leather preserving products. Many horses and people show skin irritation to modern cleaners, and simple soap and warm water is often the safe option. Before using any new product on the horse's skin it is best to do a spot test. A small amount of the substance is placed on a non-hairy area (inner thigh) and examined after a couple of hours to see if there is any inflammation (redness).

Flies are a seasonal problem. They annoy the animal by swarming around its head and feeding on the discharges from the eyes and nostrils. Some give painful bites and are blood sucking. Horses may be allergic to the bites of certain insects, the commonest being the allergy to midge bites, Sweet itch.

It is important to use fly repellents and/or insecticides before the horse is bitten. Horses can be stabled when the flies are most active. Fly

Acquired marks shown as patches of white hair

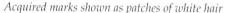

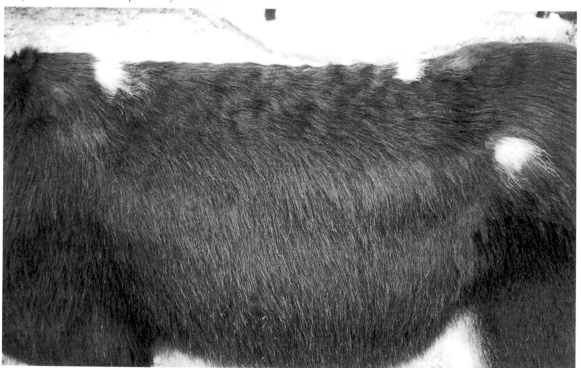

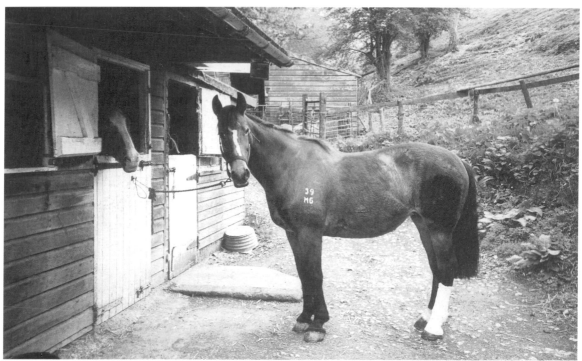

A freeze mark on the shoulder

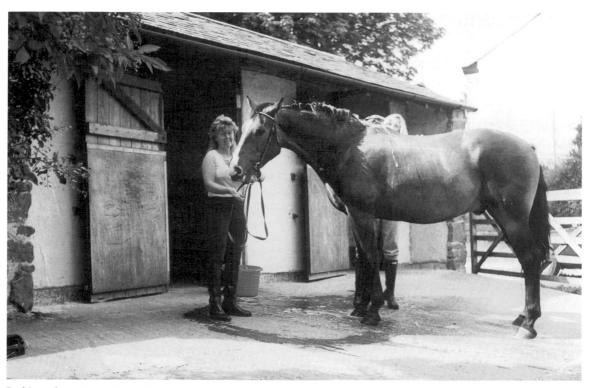

Bathing a horse (C. L. Hocking)

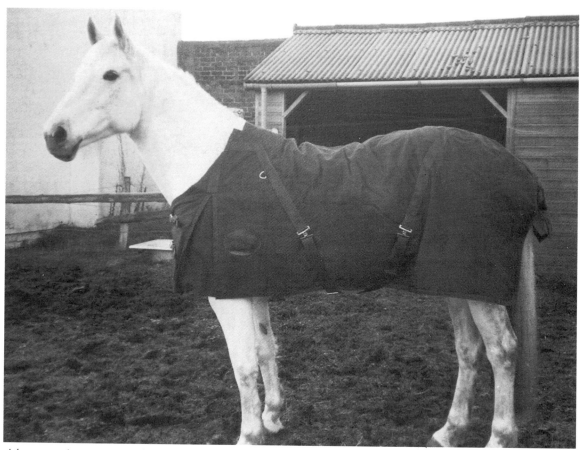

A horse wearing a waterproof outdoor rug

fringes and veils are useful but may become caught on fencing or branches, so must be used with care and closely supervised. Lightweight rugs (summer sheets) will keep the flies off the horse while it is in the stable and the removal of manure heaps from stable areas will also reduce the number of flies. Some insecticides are oily, pour-on products (permethrin) which are active for several weeks providing they are not washed off. These also kill lice so are used in the autumn/winter. The aromatic fly repellents tend to be short acting so these have to be frequently applied.

Shelter should be provided from strong sunlight as well as flies. Animals with unpigmented muzzles are prone to sunburn and need protection with a high factor sun screen.

Wet cold weather can also cause problems for the skin, e.g. rainscald and mud rash. These can be prevented by providing a field shelter with a hard standing and by using waterproof rugs and avoiding turn-out pastures which are poorly drained.

GROOMING AND SKIN CARE CHECKLIST

* look for injuries and first signs of disease
* wash grooming kits frequently
* keep tack clean and in good repair
* wash rugs and numnahs in non-detergents and rinse well
* test shampoos and sheath cleaners before use
* use fly and external parasite control
* use sunscreen on unpigmented skin
* prevent the skin becoming too wet

ROUTINE DENTAL CHECKS

Domesticated horses need routine dental care. They are given diets which modify their eating patterns. They have bits in their mouths from a young age and are not selectively bred for good dentition or even wear of cheek teeth. Animals which have slight abnormalities at eight years old may have a serious problem by their mid teens if they do not receive corrective dentistry at a young age. Preventive dentistry is vital as the condition of the horse's teeth is very important with regard to its health and welfare. The equine evolved as a grazing animal, normally spending eight to fourteen hours daily eating plant material. The silicates in grass are abrasive and normally wear down the teeth, acting like pumice as the horse chews. The lower jaw (mandible) of the horse is narrower (30%) than the upper jaw (maxilla). As the horse chews the sideways movement favours wear on the outside edge of the lower cheek teeth and the inside edge of the upper cheek teeth. Sharp enamel points tend to form on the outer (buccal) edge of the upper cheek teeth and on the inside (lingual) edge of the lower cheek teeth which can cause ulceration of the cheeks and tongue. Tight nosebands press the cheeks against the sharp points and cause pain and discomfort when tacked up.

The horse has both deciduous (milk) and permanent teeth. At about nine months old the foal will have a full set of deciduous teeth; these include six front (incisor) teeth and six premolar (cheek) teeth in the maxilla and mandible. The gap between the incisors and the cheek teeth is the interdental space or bars. The incisors are small and white and rounded at the gum margin. The middle incisors are referred to as the centrals, the teeth on either side are the laterals and

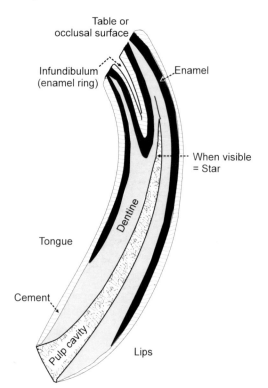

Fig.10. Section through lower incisor tooth.

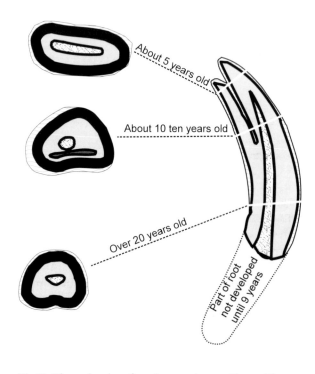

Fig.11. The occlusal surface changes shape with age. The infundibulum becomes shallow and the dental star appears.

A healthy horse at grass

the teeth on the outside of these are the corner incisors.

The eruption times for temporary teeth in foals are:

0–1 week	central incisors
4–6 weeks	lateral incisors
6–9 months	corner incisors
0–2 weeks	1st, 2nd and 3rd premolars (left and right side upper and lower jaw)

There are twenty-four milk teeth.

The bones of the head expand during the next two years and allow room for thirty-six to forty-four adult teeth. The changes continue at a slower rate throughout the horse's life as the permanent teeth continue to erupt their reserve crowns. These are hypsodont teeth, i.e. most of the crown (80 to 90 mm) is under the gum in the jaw bone in the young horse. The root is short and slow to form (six to nine years). The teeth continue to erupt 2 to 3 mm per year as the occlusal (biting) surface wears away. Because of this continuous wear and eruption any misalignment or disease can affect the function of the cheek teeth.

The permanent (adult) incisor teeth erupt at specific times in most horses. The centrals at $2\frac{1}{2}$ years, the laterals at $3\frac{1}{2}$ years and the corners at $4\frac{1}{2}$ years. The teeth in the upper jaw are larger and erupt before those in the lower jaw. They are in wear (attrition) with those of the opposite jaw approximately six months after erupting. The permanent incisors are large teeth, yellow in colour and square at the gum margin. The eruption times for the larger breeds, e.g. shires, Warmbloods are later than the thoroughbred.

Traditionally, horses have been 'aged' by examining the incisor teeth but recent research

A four-year-old

23

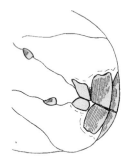
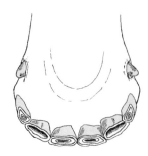

Fig.12. Four-year-old.

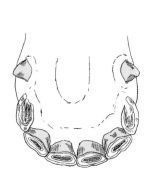

Fig.13. Five-year-old.

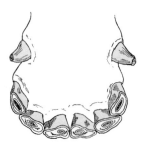

Fig.14. Eight-year-old.

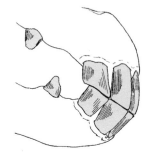
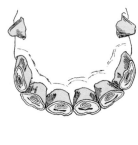

Fig.15. Nine-year-old.

has revealed that this is an inaccurate method of ageing animals over six years of age. The eruption of the permanent incisor teeth gives a fairly accurate correlation with the actual age of the horse but the ageing of older animals becomes less precise with increasing age and is no more than an 'informed' guess!

There are twenty-four cheek teeth in the permanent dentition, six on either side of the upper and lower jaws, three premolars and three molars. The premolars (PM) and molars (M) of the upper jaw are broad and square; the lower cheek teeth are narrower and rectangular. The grinding surfaces have ridges of cement, enamel and dentine which are sharp and serrated.

The cheek teeth are numbered 1 to 6 from the bar to the angle of the jaw. They erupt at $2\frac{1}{2}$ years, 3 years, 4 years, 1 year, 2 years and $3\frac{1}{2}$ years. The first three permanent cheek teeth may have the remains of the temporary premolar teeth (retained caps) stuck on top of them.

Male horses normally have two upper and two lower canine teeth which erupt at four years of age in each interdental space. Canines are absent or rudimentary in mares.

Some horses have a small vestigial tooth (wolf tooth) just in front of the first cheek tooth. They vary in position, root length and angle. There may be one to four of these teeth. Occasionally wolf teeth cause a problem in which case they are removed.

The eruption times for permanent teeth are:

$2\frac{1}{2}$ years central incisors
$3\frac{1}{2}$ years lateral incisors
$4\frac{1}{2}$ years corner incisors
4–5 years canines

PERMANENT CHEEK TEETH

1	2	3	4	5	6
PM2	PM3	PM4	M1	M2	M3
$2\frac{1}{2}$yr	3yr	4yr	1yr	2yr	$3\frac{1}{2}$–4yr

As you can see the first cheek tooth is the second premolar, the wolf tooth is the first premolar tooth.

There is a method used to number the teeth so that there is no confusion about which tooth is

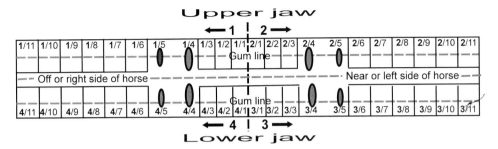

First number (**1 - 4**) defines Quadrant

Second number (1 - 11) defines tooth ⟶ 1 - 3 = incisors
4 = canines
5 = wolf teeth
6 -8 = premolars
9 - 11 = molars

Fig. 16. Dentition numbering system

under treatment. The mouth is divided into quadrants, i.e. upper right is number 1, upper left is number 2, lower left is number 3 and lower right is number 4. When facing the horse the numbers go clockwise. Each tooth is then given a number 1 to 11. The central incisor being 1 and the last cheek tooth 11 in each quadrant. To locate a tooth first state the number for the jaw and then the tooth number, e.g. 3.4 is the canine tooth on the lower left.

See chart above.

The dental examination

All horses require a dental examination every six months with any required dental maintenance carried out. Foals should be examined for congenital defects of the lips, palate and tongue. Some foals have dental malocclusions of the incisor teeth (parrot mouth), i.e. the upper jaw is longer than the lower jaw so the incisor teeth are not opposed. This condition should be corrected in the young foal to prevent problems later on. A bracing apparatus is used to slow down the growth rate of the upper jaw allowing the lower jaw to catch up in length. At six to eight months old all the incisors will have erupted and the occlusion of incisors and premolars should be checked. The premolars must be checked for sharp points and the tongue and cheeks for ulcers.

Over the next four years all sorts of changes are occurring in the mouth of the young horse. Teeth are erupting and being lost. Up to 60% of two to four year olds will suffer from gingivitis (gum inflammation). The mouth should be examined for wolf teeth; bit injuries on the bars and corners of the mouth; enamel points on cheek teeth; hooks on PM2 and M3; retained

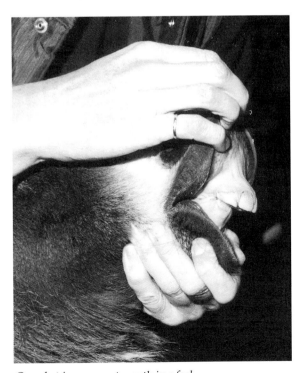

Overshot jaw – parrot mouth in a foal

25

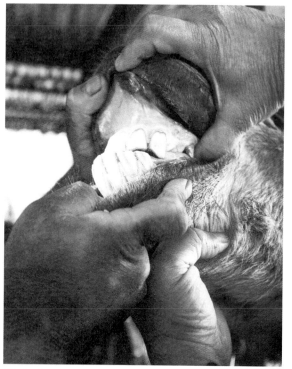

Undershot jaw

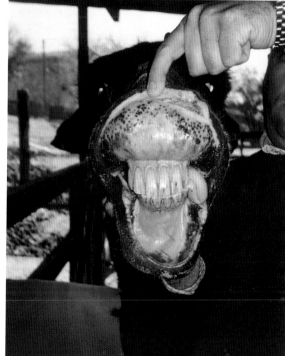

An injury to the inside of the upper lip

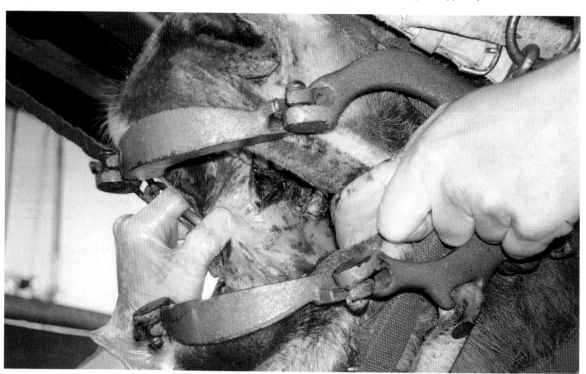

A large hook on the 1/6 right upper cheek tooth

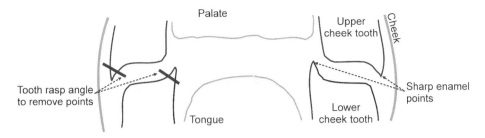

Fig.17. Sharp enamel points on the outer edge of the upper molars and the inner edge of the lower molar teeth.

caps. Incisors should be checked for retained or extra teeth. By five years all the incisors and canines should have erupted so they can be visually examined and palpated for sharp edges and tartar. Occasionally too many teeth may be present or teeth can erupt in the wrong position. The molar teeth also must be checked for good alignment and proper eruption. Horses with small dished heads have more curve to the jaws and are more prone to overcrowding of teeth than horses with long roman noses and straight dental arcades.

The horse's diet plays a major role in the wear of the cheek teeth. The amount of lateral movement of the lower jaw depends on the length of forage. Feeding pellets and short length forage

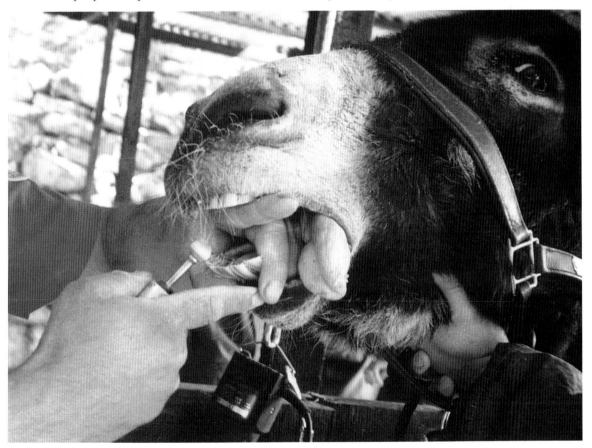

Using a dremel to balance incisor teeth

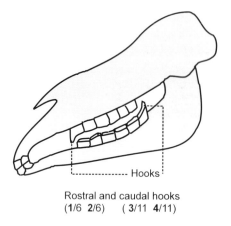

Rostral and caudal hooks
(1/6 **2/6**)   (**3/11** 4/11)

Fig.18. Rostral and caudal hooks on 1/6, 2/6, 3/11, 4/11.

limits the jaw movement and causes the formation of sharp points. Horses at pasture or fed hay or straw have a wide range of jaw movement. Malocclusions of incisors and molars will cause abnormal patterns of wear which lead to serious dental problems. Hooks can occur on the first upper cheek tooth and the last lower cheek tooth. These can become long and pointed and meet the opposite soft tissue and lock the jaws as any sideways movement is painful.

Pain will alter chewing movements so abnormal wear occurs. Food material may become packed around the molar teeth causing gingivitis and peridontitis (inflammation of the tooth socket). The teeth may become loose especially in elderly horses. If a tooth is lost the opposing tooth becomes too long and prevents normal chewing. Overlong teeth have to be cut off with shears or rasped frequently.

Infection of the tooth roots of the upper cheek teeth may result in facial swelling and an offensive nasal discharge if the tooth root abscess bursts into the sinus cavity. Abscess of the lower molar roots causes a swelling and pus/scabs on the lower jaw bone. Young horses often have a bumpy lower jaw when the teeth are erupting.

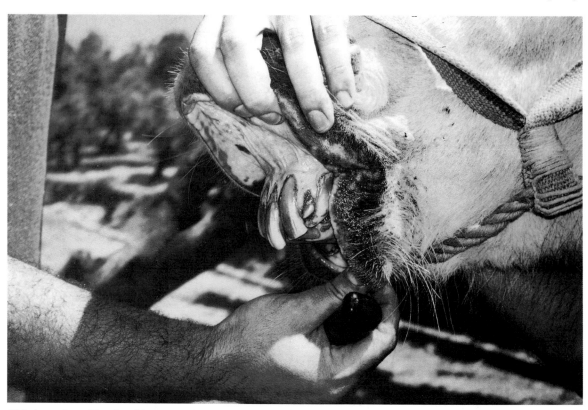

Elderly equine with splayed incisor teeth

Fig.19. Late teens.

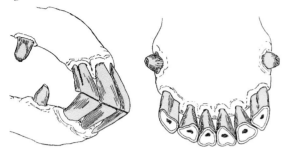

Fig.20. Twenty plus.

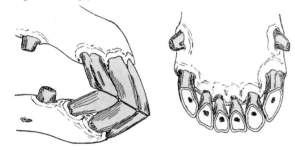

Teeth with root abscesses used to be removed but recently drilling out the root and using amalgam has been tried as an alternative treatment, which if successful saves the tooth. Signs of dental disease are:

poor bodily condition
slow to finish food
quidding (dropping chewed food out of mouth)
food pouched in the cheeks
salivating
abnormal chewing action
facial swelling
smelly nasal discharge from one nostril
halitosis (bad breath)
colic and choke due to inadequately chewed feed
abnormal head carriage when ridden, headshaking
reluctance to drink cold water
whole grain or long stems in faeces

Usually a gag (a full mouth speculum) is placed in the horse's mouth so that all the teeth can be fully inspected. The horse has to be adequately restrained or in some cases sedated. If

Sinus infection treated by trephining (C. L. Hocking)

A dental gag is used to hold the mouth open

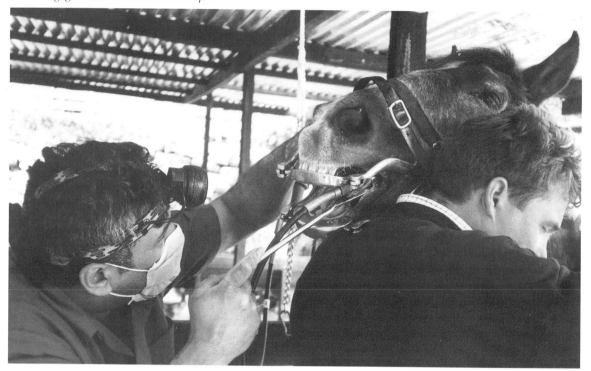

The use of a dental rasp

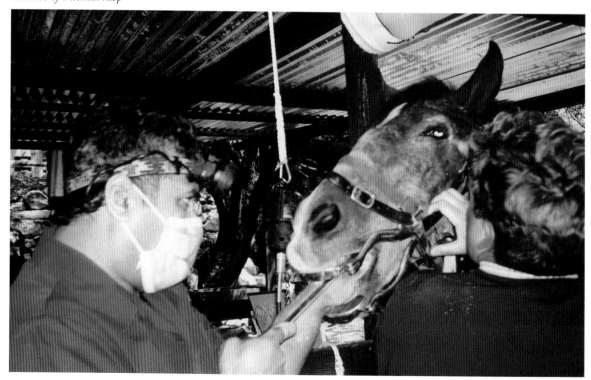

Failure of teeth 4/2 and 4/3 to erupt

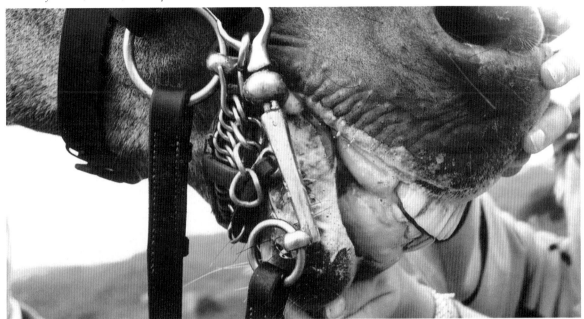

extensive surgery is required the horse will be anaesthetised. X-rays of the head are useful if infection of the sinuses is suspected or the position of a root has to be located in an abnormal eruption site.

Only veterinary surgeons are qualified and legally allowed to remove teeth and sedate horses. Many lay dental technicians rasp teeth but some have no training while others have qualified and trained in the U.S.A. There will be a recognised training course with certification in the U.K. for Equine Dental Technicians in the near future.

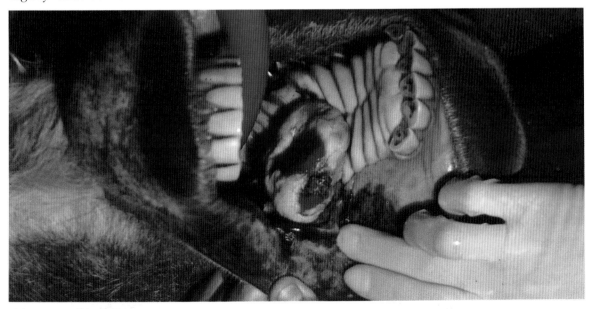

A tumour on the palate

FOOT CARE

The foot is a common site of disease and injury. Feet should be carefully inspected every day. They should be picked out morning and evening and before and after exercise. Horses out at grass need to have their feet attended to at least once a day. Hoof picks which have a brush at one end are useful.

The horse should be tied up and standing square with its weight taken equally on all limbs. If the feet are picked out in the same order each time the horse will soon learn the routine and there will be no reluctance to have the feet picked up. The limb joints should bend easily in a normal healthy animal. The clean hoof wall is checked for damage, e.g. cracks or horn deficits. The sole is cleaned and should be free of any sensitive or sore areas. The grooves on either side of the frog and the central sulcus are easy to clean with a brush. Any grit is removed from the white line. The heels and the coronary band are checked for injuries. The temperature of the feet will vary throughout the day and warm feet do not always signify disease (a consistently hot foot with a bounding digital pulse is a sign of inflammation within the hoof).

If the horse is shod the position and wear on the shoe is checked, and the clenches are felt to make sure they are tight against the hoof wall.

Raised clenches can cause injuries to the opposite limb especially in animals who do not have a straight action. Any soil or stones are removed from under the shoe at the heels and between the shoe and the sole.

In dry, hot conditions the hoof dries out so it is important to wet the feet to prevent the horn becoming brittle and cracked. In wet conditions the hoof can become saturated, however wet feet will soon dry out in a clean shavings bed.

FOOT EXAMINATION CHECKLIST

Examine wall for defects
Examine frog and sole for injuries
Check heels and coronary band
Note position of shoe, state of wear and feel the clenches

The horse's diet, state of health, environmental factors, climate, and farriery all affect the quality and rate of hoof horn growth. Horn growth rate slows down in cold, dry conditions and increases in warm, moist conditions. Good quality horn can withstand environmental challenges and protect the pedal bone from concussion. Some animals inherit poor quality horn, with crumbly

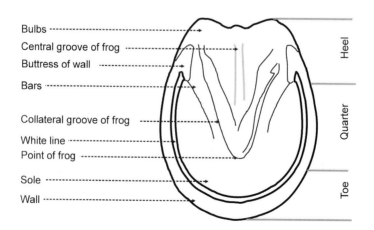

Bulbs
Central groove of frog
Buttress of wall
Bars
Collateral groove of frog
White line
Point of frog
Sole
Wall

Heel
Quarter
Toe

Fig.21. Structures on the ground surface of a hind foot.

walls and thin soles; these animals should not be bred from. Poor quality horn is susceptible to many diseases and also predisposes to pedal bone damage (pedal osteitis).

Dietary factors

Ideally a horse on a balanced diet which includes good quality forage should have all the necessary nutrients to grow good horn. Often diets which lack calcium and protein result in poor horn tubule formation. Occasionally inadequate levels of biotin will cause horn defects. Feeding bran was historically a common cause of calcium deficiency in the diet, however today bran is not such a popular part of the horse's diet, being replaced by forage such as chopped hay, straw and alfalfa mixes. Alfalfa is a good source of both calcium – in a form which can be absorbed by the horse's gut – and protein. Sugar beet and carrots are also a good source of calcium. The calcium in limestone is not as easily absorbed and is therefore not the best way of giving extra calcium to equines. There are a number of dietary supplements on the market which are supposed to promote hoof horn growth rate and quality. They have not all been scientifically tested so it is best to ask veterinary or farriery advice before purchasing such products.

Environmental factors

Horses kept in very wet conditions with no chance for the feet to dry out will be prone to horn infections, e.g. thrush or hollow hoof disease. Wet horn is weaker than dry horn and the hoof loses its shape. The walls flare and separate, the heels collapse and the sole becomes flatter and thicker. The toes become long and the minerals are leached out of the hoof. Keratolytic (horn destroying) bacteria and fungi can enter the hoof through defects in the horn.

Ammonia from urine in deep litter beds will damage the horn, chemicals like formalin, copper sulphate and strong disinfectants are all detrimental to hoof horn and should be avoided.

Hoof oils, creams and tars will trap the excessive moisture in the hoof and provide an ideal environment for anaerobic infections.

Ideally the hoof should not need any dressing other than to be washed with clean water. The outer surface of the hoof is naturally shiny and protects the inner layers. The modern hoof dressings are designed to allow air and moisture in and out of the horn and protect it from ammonia in the bedding, so maintaining good quality horn.

Farriery

Many domesticated horses live in a confined area so that hoof growth rate exceeds hoof wear. The hoof wall grows 8 to 10 mm per month on average. Horses in work are shod to prevent excessive wear on the hoof wall. Most horses will need their hooves trimmed at four to six week intervals. The farrier will advise on the trimming interval for each individual animal and this may alter from summer to winter when climatic and diet changes affect horn growth rate.

Overlong feet cause lameness and distortion of the hoof. The bones, joints, ligaments and tendons

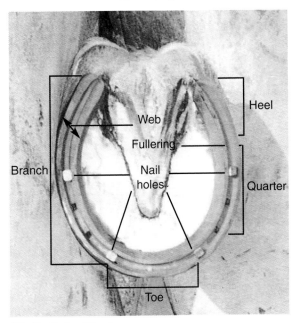

Fig.22. Parts of the shoe

Fig.23. Section through a horse's foot.

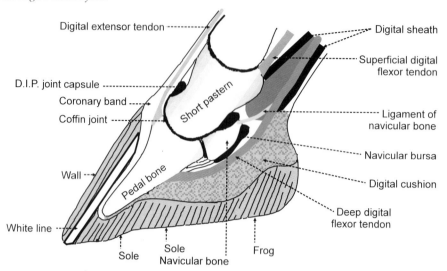

higher up the limb are also put under abnormal stresses which can result in long-term lameness. Shoes which are left on too long will have raised clenches. The shoe moves off the wall onto the sole, causing bruising and corns. The shoe may be pulled off and cause further damage if areas of wall are torn away or if the horse punctures the foot on a nail.

It is the responsibility of the owner to make regular appointments with the farrier. In order for the farrier to do a professional job he needs certain conditions to work in:

A clean dry horse with the feet picked out
The horse should be correctly restrained and be used to having its feet handled
A well lit shoeing area with a smooth flat surface to walk the horse on to check foot balance

The farrier is trained to trim the feet, to prepare them for shoes and to fit the shoes. They are trained in the anatomy of the limbs and feet, horsemanship and metal-work. Many are experienced in radiology, lameness diagnosis and disease processes. Some farriers specialise in surgical shoeing when they work closely with their veterinary colleagues. Many foot lamenesses involve both veterinary and farriery expertise as well as owner co-operation. Often the farrier is the first person to detect a problem. Abnormal wear on the shoe may be the first sign of an alter-

ation in gait due to a lameness. Reluctance to bend a joint during shoeing may be an early sign of arthritic pain. As the farrier sees the horse at frequent intervals he will notice weight changes and will also be aware of any infectious diseases in the area.

Shoes may be metal or plastic, handmade or machine-made (keg), they may be attached to the wall by nails or by glues. Aluminium shoes are lighter than steel shoes but not as hard wearing. The farrier decides which type of shoe to use on a particular animal. The amount and type of work has to be considered as well as the quality of the hoof wall and its ability to hold the nails. Horses with abnormal foot flight patterns or those which forge, overreach or brush may need special shoeing to prevent further problems. By careful foot balance and shoeing some toe-in or toe-out conformation can be improved.

Foot balance

In order to balance the feet the farrier assesses the conformation of the horse, paying special attention to the limbs and the hooves. The shape of the hoof capsule, the length of the toe and the thickness of the horn on the sole, frog and bars must all be considered prior to trimming to a

Fig.24. Assessing foot balance.

(a) *a perpendicular line from the point of shoulder should bisect the knee, fetlock pastern and hoof.*

(b) *The hoof pastern axis is parallel to the heel and the middle of P1, P2 and P3. A line from the centre of the coffin joint divides the hoof in half.*

(c) *A line down the centre of the cannon bone is at right angles to the pastern and heels if the foot is balanced medio-laterally.*

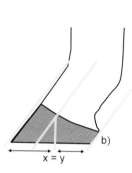

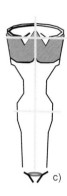

correct shape. The front feet should be a matching pair, as should the hind feet. The front feet are rounder than the hind feet. The soles should be concave and thick enough to prevent bruising under normal conditions. The wall is thickest at the toe, and thinner at the heels.

When viewed from the side the hoof wall at the toe should be parallel to the hoof wall at the heel and parallel to the slope of the shoulder. The hoof pastern axis should be a straight line and not broken. If the hoof pastern axis is broken the slope on the pastern is not the same as the slope on the hoof wall. A broken hoof pastern axis should be restored by correctly trimming the hoof.

The normal angle between the hoof wall and the ground is 45 to 50 degrees for front feet and 50 to 55 degrees for hind feet. There is a lot of individual variation but the angle should be the same as that of the pastern and shoulder in the normal horse. Horses with long, sloping pasterns put more strain on their suspensory ligament, flexor tendons and sesamoid bones. Horses with upright pasterns suffer from increased concussion to their pastern and fetlock joints and are predisposed to arthritic conditions and navicular disease.

Medio-lateral balance (inside-outside) means that the foot lands flat on the ground as the walls are the same height. This is checked by picking up the foot and letting the leg hang under the horse in a natural way, holding the leg by the front of the cannon bone. By viewing across the heels it is easy to see if they are the same height

Fig.25. Broken back hoof pastern axis (HPA).

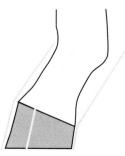

Fig.26. Broken forward hoof pastern axis.

and at right angles to a line down the centre of the flexor tendons. A 'T' square placed over the middle of the flexor tendons should have the right-angled bar level with the weight-bearing surface of a correctly balanced foot. (See page 102.)

Medio-lateral imbalances are common and cause quarter cracks and twisting of the hoof capsule, arthritic lower limb joints and dishing. In the front feet the outside toe quarter is often left long so the horse lands on this part of the wall and then crushes down onto the inside heel. The inside wall becomes straighter and the heel becomes jammed up. The outside wall will eventually become convex and the heels may shear apart so the feet appear pigeon-toed. In the hind feet the converse is true with the inside wall left long so the outside heel is the second impact site and the hind feet will turn out. It is very impor-tant that the feet are balanced correctly otherwise the horse will show lameness due to foot and limb pain.

When viewed from the front the feet should not turn inwards (pigeon-toe) or point outwards (splay foot). The whole limb may deviate or the problem may occur low down, e.g. deviation at the fetlock or pastern. With a toe-in conformation the foot usually swings outwards (paddles); with toe-out the foot swings inwards (wings) and damages the opposite leg.

The horse should be walked and trotted in hand so that the limb flight patterns can be assessed. Sometimes the limbs interfere with each other, causing brushing and overreach injuries. Animals with poor limb conformation will have poor foot conformation due to abnormal stresses on the hoof capsule.

FEEDING

Horses and ponies are herbivores. They evolved to eat plants like grasses and coarse vegetation, not lush fertilised pasture land. Feral horses spend up to 16 hours a day grazing. Their teeth and digestive tract are designed to utilise a forage diet. They also have a psychological need to spend time searching for and chewing forage. Animals fed on concentrate diets which can be eaten three to six times faster than the same weight of fibre are more likely to exhibit stereotypic behaviour (boredom vices). Forage is an essential part of the equine diet to maintain the teeth and guts in good order and for the mental well-being of the animal. Although many animals only require a forage diet, those in hard

work, young growing animals, breeding stock, the ill or elderly may require concentrates and supplements in addition to the forage.

Horses are fed forage (grass, hay, straw), cereals (oats, barley, maize) and other straights like soaked sugar beet and compound feeds such as pellets and coarse mixes.

Water is also an essential nutrient and without it a horse will soon become dehydrated, seriously ill and may die. The volume of water required by a horse depends on the moisture content of the feed, the size of the animal, the amount of exercise taken and the weather conditions.

Foods vary in their water content; grass contains 80% water, compounds and hay may only

Fig.27. Common varieties of grasses.

Offering water during a fun ride

salts like electrolytes to water may stop a horse from drinking. Insufficient water will lead to a depressed appetite and weight loss and dry gut contents which may cause impactions and colic. The basic nutrients provided by a balanced feed are carbohydrates as starch and fibre; protein and fat. Vitamins and minerals are also needed in small amounts for a variety of bodily functions. Forage such as grass and hay can provide all the nutrients a horse needs. The composition of grass alters through the growing season. Young grass is high in nutrients, especially soluble carbohydrates and only has a small amount of fibre. As the grass matures it has longer stems and less leaf and has a lower nutrient value.

The feed value of hay will vary depending on how well it was made and what species of grass it contains. Once the grass has been cut for hay it may deteriorate if it is rained on and it can become mouldy if it takes a long time to dry. Barn dried hay will contain more minerals, vitamins and other nutrients than hay made on the field.

There are alternative packaged feeds to hay which may be more expensive but have the advantage of being dust free, clean and of known nutritional value. These include haylage, short chop hay and straw chaffs, high fibre pellets and alfalfa.

Horses that need more energy than a forage diet can supply require energy feed such as cereals, either fed as individual grains (straights) or mixed in commercial compound feeds as pellets or coarse mixes.

Cereals can be fed as whole grains, rolled, extruded or micronised. Cereals commonly fed to horses are oats, barley and maize. Wheat by-products, bran and breadcrumbs are also fed. Cereals are usually mixed with other ingredients to give a balanced diet. As most owners are not experts in nutrition it is safer to use a commercially formulated compound feed to supplement the forage ration. There are compound feeds to suit all age groups and types of performance horse. These have been expertly designed by the equine nutritionist employed by the manufacturer. Most companies have an advice helpline for their customers and as with all products you get

contain 15% moisture. Horses on a high protein diet will drink more water and produce more urine.

A 500 kg horse at rest requires 25 lit (5 gal) of water. Exercise in hot conditions may increase the water requirement three-fold to 75 lit (15 gal). Water is lost from the body in urine, faeces, sweat and from the respiratory tract.

Horses should always have access to clean, fresh water and this must be checked twice a day. Water may be provided in clean buckets, troughs, automatic drinking bowls or from streams or ponds. Natural supplies may dry up in summer-time or become stagnant. In the winter water may freeze over and access to streams may be very muddy and dangerous. Many horses have been stuck in ponds and streams. Bucket handles and sharp edges on troughs can cause injuries. Old baths are often used as water containers and can cause horrific injuries, especially when headcollars are caught on taps. The newer rubber-type water troughs are the safest option in fields. Most horses prefer cool, clean water and are reluctant to drink tainted water. Adding

Filling hay nets in the feed store

Feed scoops come in various shapes and sizes so you need to know how much by weight each scoop holds.

The horse's gut contains billions of friendly bacteria that assist the digestion of plant material. These bacteria can be destroyed by sudden changes in the diet, especially high cereal and starch rich food which alter the acidity of the gut contents. This can cause laminitis, colic and digestive upsets such as diarrhoea and flatulence. All changes in diet should be made slowly and for a good reason – do not swap and change your horse's diet just to feed what happens to be in fashion! If your horse is healthy, the correct weight, i.e. condition score 3 and works well you do not need to change the diet. If you need advice related to feeding ask the expert, not the next door neighbour! Remember over 75% of the horses in the UK are overweight so a lot of money is being wasted on feed.

The amount that the horse needs to eat depends on a number of factors. Firstly the size of the horse, not only its height and present weight but also the condition score. The type of work done or exercise taken and the frequency of exercise will affect its energy requirements. It is a common fault to overestimate workload. Most animals are at maintenance or a light level of work. This would be hacking three or four times a week and out at pasture each day. Show jumping and dressage competition horses that are worked six days a week would have a medium workload. Hunting, endurance work and eventing would be classed as hard work. The daily ration is then divided into a percentage of roughage and a percentage of concentrates depending on workload.

Horses on maintenance exercise need 100% of the ration as forage. Horses in light work need 80 to 85% ration as forage and 15 to 20% as concentrates. Horses in medium work need 75% forage and 25% concentrates.

The horse's management system also has to be considered. The horse may have access to grazing all or part of the day, which may be a lush meadow or poor scrubland. Horses that are rugged up and provided with a field shelter require less calories to maintain their body

what you pay for. It is false economy to go for the cheaper feeds which may contain poor quality ingredients and may not be as accurately analysed and formulated.

The vitamin and mineral supplements are added to the mixes and pellets and providing they are consumed before the 'use by' date on the label do not add further supplements to a balanced feed. The label will also list the nutrients in the feed and the batch number, 'sell by' date and suggested amounts to feed.

Horses have small stomachs and are naturally trickle feeders, which means that they need frequent small feeds. Roughage is given to dilute the compound feeds and prevent digestive disturbances. All food should be fed by weight. Hay can be weighed in a net using a balance scale.

weight than those without rugs and shelters. Animals that are clipped out may be stabled most of the time. Weather conditions will also affect the way food is utilised. The digestion of roughage is thermogenic, i.e. it produces heat. If a number of animals are fed hay in the field it may be difficult to monitor the amount each individual receives. Obviously animals on an inadequate worming programme and those with dental problems will not utilise the food properly. Animals that are debilitated, stressed or in pain may lose weight on what seems to be an adequate ration. The temperament of the horse should also be considered as this may affect the type of feed you use.

As a rough rule of thumb and a starting point in calculating the amount of food your horse requires, first calculate its body-weight. There are a number of weight bands on the market that give an estimated weight on the heart girth measurement. These vary in accuracy depending on the height and type of horse; most are accurate to

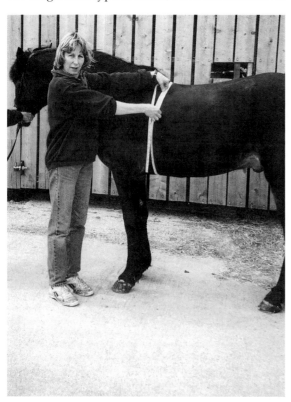

Heart girth measurement

within 3 to 10% of the actual body weight. Horses normally eat 2 to 2½% of their body weight each day. A 500 kg horse will require 10 to 12½ kg per day. Donkeys and native ponies require less than 2% to remain at their present weight. If your horse or pony is overweight it is getting too much food and in order to lose weight it needs less calories and more exercise. Calculate its ideal weight and feed at 75% requirement for that weight in order to lose some kilos. It is a lot easier to put weight on than to lose it. It is important to recognise small fluctuations in weight so the diet can be altered before the animal is grossly under or overweight. Heart girth measurements taken at fortnightly intervals are an easy way to monitor body-weight changes. All animals are individuals so the diet that suits one may not suit another.

Feeding guidelines:

1 Fresh clean water should always be available.
2 Feed according to body-weight and work load.
3 Feed small amounts at regular intervals. Keep to a routine.
4 Feed hay before and after concentrates. Mix chaff with concentrates.
5 Weigh all food and keep a record.
6 Changes in diet must be gradual to allow the gut bacteria to adjust and prevent illness.
7 Use good quality food and avoid dusty, mouldy hay.
8 Store feed in vermin-proof, labelled bins in a cool, dry building. Store hay and straw on pallets.
9 Keep all utensils, buckets and mangers clean. Provide each horse with its own equipment.
10 Monitor body-weight and condition score frequently.
11 Feed balanced rations. Do not overdose vitamins and minerals.
12 Do not feed or give large volumes of water immediately before or after exercise.
13 Give carrots or apples to stabled horses that have no grass.

Vitamins

Vitamins belong to the water-soluble group, e.g. B complex and C or the fat soluble group, e.g. A, D, E, K which are stored in the liver and body fat. The bacteria in the horse's gut make the B vitamins and vitamin K. Vitamin C is produced in

Vitamin	Source	Required for
A	Grass new hay, carrots Green food, alfalfa	Nerve function, immune system, eye sight
B	Forage and grains, synthesized in the gut	General metabolism of fats, carbohydrates and protein, skin repair and haemoglobin
C	Synthesized in the body	Muscle function, immunity
D	Sun cured forage, fish oil, synthesized in the skin	Bone formation, calcium and phosphorus metabolism
E	Green forage and cereals	Muscle function, fat metabolism

the liver and Vitamin D is formed in the skin when it is exposed to sunlight. In the winter Vitamin A and D reserves may be depleted and supplementation may be needed. The horse is unlikely to need extra B vitamins unless the gut flora is upset after antibiotic treatment or sudden changes in diet. Young, sick and stressed animals need an increased level of vitamins. Healthy adult horses fed on good quality, correctly stored rations are unlikely to need extra vitamins. Excess amounts of water-soluble vitamins are excreted from the body, unlike the fat-soluble vitamins which are toxic if overdosed.

Minerals

Minerals, unlike some of the vitamins cannot be synthesised in the animal's body; they have to be supplied in the diet. The main minerals are Calcium, Phosphorus, Magnesium, Sodium, Potassium and Chlorine. There are a number of trace elements which are needed in small amounts. These include Iron, Copper, Zinc, Manganese, Cobalt, Iodine and Selenium.

Compound feeds already contain minerals and trace elements in the correct proportions. Horses that are on a purely forage diet of grass and hay can be given a forage balancer. Salt licks can also contain minerals as well as sodium chloride.

There are a plethora of herbal and other supplements or additives on the market, all claiming to have beneficial effects, but most have never been scientifically tested. They are not subject to rigorous analysis like medicines and may contain unwanted impurities. They are sometimes thought to cure conditions or alleviate symptoms but this is based mainly on results on human experience. Think carefully before you buy supplements for your horse, be sure that it is needed and that it is safe to use.

Mineral	Source	Used for
Calcium	Alfalfa Sugar beet Carrots Milk	Bone structure, muscle and nerve function
Phosphorus	Cereals	Same as above
Magnesium	Bran Vegetables Milk	Bones and teeth structure, muscle function Electrolyte balance
Sodium Chlorine Potassium	Forage Hay Grass	Maintaining pH, electrolyte balance, nerve and muscle function

EXERCISE

Exercise is important for both the physical and mental well-being of the horse. This may be unsupervised walking in the field while grazing or, at the opposite end of the scale, the hard work and high level of schooling performed by the elite athlete. Most equines are kept for pleasure and leisure pursuits, not serious competition, so their workload is light. It is good to consider where, when and how much work you should give your horse. The work should not cause injuries like sprains or strains nor cause exhaustion or illness. Animals that are inadequately prepared for exercise by not having been properly warmed up, or those which become tired are more likely to sustain injuries. Most injuries occur due to unfitness; poor conformation; incorrect tack; poor conditions underfoot; rider inexperience and accidents. The correct tack should be used for the type of work and it should fit correctly. Badly fitting tack causes pain and injuries

and affects the horse's attitude to work. Interference injuries like brushing and over-reaching are seen in young unbalanced animals, tired animals and those with poor limb conformation. Exercise boots must be fitted carefully to avoid them slipping down or causing pressure injuries if too tightly applied.

The ability of the rider will reflect the type of terrain and activity the horse can cope with. An inexperienced rider may cause an accident by poor balance, errors in judgement and physically hindering the horse. They will certainly come to grief on a novice or young horse if they overestimate their riding prowess. Inexperienced riders on inexperienced horses can spell disaster for the horse and ruin it for the future. Horses under four years old may not be used in riding establishments nor competed in any sport other than racing. Many horses raced as two year olds never reach maturity as they are injured.

Badly fitting boots cause injury

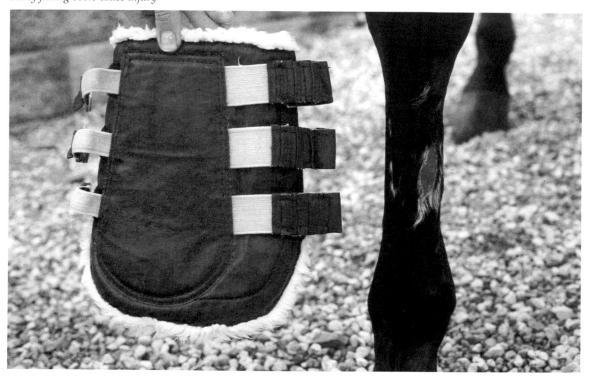

Horses wearing knee boots (C. L. Hocking)

There are advantages and disadvantages to riding on all types of terrain. Roads tend to be smooth but are a hard surface and cause concussion to the limb joints, especially in trot work. In winter the surface may be icy. Anyone who exercises horses on public roads should be aware of the Highway Code relating to horses. The British Horse Society holds training courses and Road Safety tests for horse-riders. It is important to be clearly visible to other road users by wearing reflective and fluorescent clothing and it is not advisable to ride on the highway at dusk or in the dark, even with stirrup lights. Horses should wear knee boots for road work and be well shod. Worn shoes should be replaced. The volume of motorised traffic even on country lanes means that the rider has to pay attention at all times to avoid accidents.

Bridleways and tracks avoid the hazards of traffic but the surfaces may be very muddy, uneven, rocky and hard. Horses may stumble, especially if ridden at speed on an unsuitable surface. Prepared surfaces like sand and wood chip are ideal for schooling the horse. They should not be too deep nor too hard. Some surfaces are springy and others are 'dead'. Pasture-land is fine to ride on at certain times of the year, when it is not baked hard or waterlogged. The type of terrain will dictate what pace you can ride at. Occasional ridden exercise should be slow and for short periods to avoid sore muscles, tendon and ligament injuries. The aim of training or fitness programmes for horses and humans is to prepare the musculoskeletal system and the heart and lungs for athletic work. The training will increase muscle strength, increase

Lungeing is a useful training aid

endurance and improve flexibility. Hill work is introduced gradually into a fitness programme. As the horse becomes fitter it can do faster and more collected work. Before commencing on a training programme it is a good idea to have a veterinary check-up and perhaps blood sample analysis. The horse must be in good health prior to work. Animals that are overweight or have respiratory or musculoskeletal problems will show exercise intolerance and loss of performance. Obesity can be avoided by correct feeding. Respiratory disease can be minimised by avoiding contact with infected animals, feeding

clean forage and keeping the environment free from dust, ammonia fumes and fungal spores and using vaccines and worming programmes. Muscle, tendon, ligament and other joint or bone disease should be diagnosed by a veterinary surgeon who will treat the condition. Sometimes the farrier or physiotherapist will work with the veterinary surgeon to rehabilitate the horse after an injury. The same performance tests used on human athletes are available for horses. Heart rate monitors are used to assess response to exercise, recovery time and fitness. Horses are worked on treadmills to check oxygen uptake,

Horse on a treadmill

respiratory and heart rate response to graded work, and to diagnose problems. Blood is analysed for muscle enzymes and lactate levels. The horse's gait can be studied using video cameras and force plates to detect lameness. Tendons are scanned using ultrasound to detect minute injuries. Swimming pools are also available for training and convalescing animals.

Grooming and massage to increase muscle tone followed by warm-up exercise prepares the horse for more vigorous work. A warm-up may include using heat lamps or a solarium or brisk walking and stretching exercises. Muscles work more efficiently when they are warm and when the weather is hot the horse will warm up faster.

Heart rate monitors have become more popular during training to assess improved fitness and work level. The heart rate can be measured at rest, before and after exercise using a stethoscope or by palpating a superficial artery (taking a pulse). These methods cannot be used while the horse is exercising so a heart rate monitor is used. As the horse becomes fitter the heart rate will be slower at a given running pace and will recover to the pre-exercise level in a shorter time.

After strenuous exercise there should be a period that allows the horse to stretch and relax. The horse should not show signs of dehydration, fatigue, exhaustion or exertional myopathies

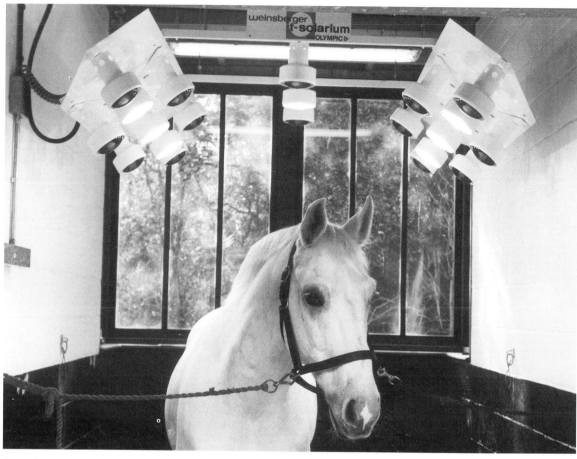

In a solarium

(tying-up). The capillary refill test and the skin pinch test, TPR and the presence of gut sounds can all be monitored.

Signs of heat stress/exhaustion/dehydration syndrome:

Reluctance to move, inco-ordination, muscle weakness and cramps
Rectal temperature over 40°C
Colic
Unwillingness to eat or drink
Sunken eyes
Depression
Rapid respiration
Pulse over 70 beats per minute
Diaphragmatic flutter (thumps)

These are all serious signs that urgent veterinary attention is needed.

Research undertaken before the Olympic games in Atlanta has shown how to cool a horse efficiently after exercising in a hot climate. The horse's normal rectal temperature at rest is 37° to 38°C (98.6° to 100.4°F). You should know your own horse's temperature. In the resting animal under moderate climatic conditions, heat is lost from the body by radiation and convection. Muscle activity during exercise produces a lot of heat which has to be removed to prevent the animal overheating. This heat is normally lost by radiation, convection and the evaporation of sweat. About 15% of heat is lost through breathing, hence the increased respiratory rate after exercise. When horses exercise in hot conditions the heat loss by radiation and convection is reduced. High humidity prevents sweat evaporating, so reducing heat loss. Excessive sweating leads to dehydration and salt imbalances. Travelling long distances can cause dehydration

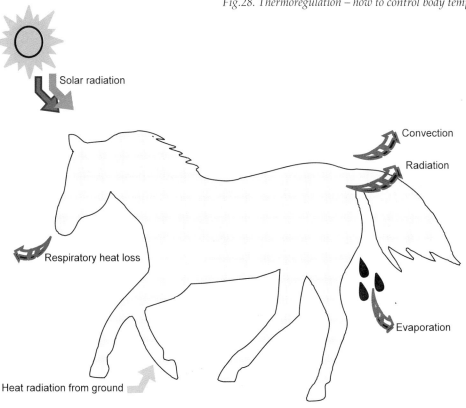

Fig.28. Thermoregulation – how to control body temperature.

Solar radiation

Convection

Radiation

Respiratory heat loss

Evaporation

Heat radiation from ground

A heart-rate monitor

so the horse may be dehydrated before exercise commences. Horses should have access to water up to 15 minutes before exercise and have hay with a hard feed at least four hours before strenuous work.

Any animal that is hot and working in a hot environment will benefit from cold water cooling. There is no evidence that cold water cooling causes tying-up.

During hot conditions you should be prepared to cool your horse and have the necessary equipment. You will need:

40 to 50 lit of ice cold water
several small buckets and large sponges
a rectal thermometer
three assistants

One person holds the horse and the other two stand either side to commence pouring cold water on all parts of the body including the hindquarters.

Horse dressed for travel (C. L. Hocking)

The tack can be left on and the temperature taken while cooling has started. Apply cold water for 30 seconds and then walk the horse for 30 seconds and then cool again, the walking between cooling is necessary as it aids evaporation and improves skin blood flow. Try to do this procedure in the shade. The horse can be offered small amounts of water to drink. The rectal temperature should decrease by 1°C every 10 minutes. When the rectal temperature reaches 38° to 39°C, the respiratory rate is less than 30 per minute, and the skin over the quarters feels cool after walking, the cooling process can stop.

There has been an increase in all types of competitions, long pleasure rides and endurance riding during the summer months so heat stress in horses is becoming more common. It is important that owners recognise this problem can occur and make every effort to avoid it. Horses and ponies that are overweight will heat up more quickly than those with less insulating fat under the skin.

PART TWO

COMMON AILMENTS

THE RESPIRATORY SYSTEM

Anatomy

The respiratory tract begins at the nostrils and ends at the alveoli (air sacs) where gaseous exchange occurs. The inspired air passes along the nasal chambers, the pharynx and larynx into the trachea. The hairs on the nostrils trap dust and dirt and prevent large particles from entering the tract. The air is also warmed and moistened as it passes over the highly vascular epithelial lining of the nasal chambers. The trachea is easy to palpate on the lower side of the neck, it is held open by a series of incomplete cartilaginous rings and is lined by a membrane which has fine hair-like projections (cilia) and mucus producing cells. Inhaled particles stick to the mucus which is propelled to the pharynx by the cilia. Obviously in the grazing animal this is also aided by gravity as the head is low. Conversely when the horse is tied with its head held up for long periods of time this reduces the clearance rate of mucus. There are also groups of lymphoid cells scattered throughout the airways. These cells maintain the lungs' defence mechanism to infectious diseases. The trachea divides into the two main bronchi inside the chest at the level of the fifth rib above the heart. The right lung is larger than the left as the heart is situated on the

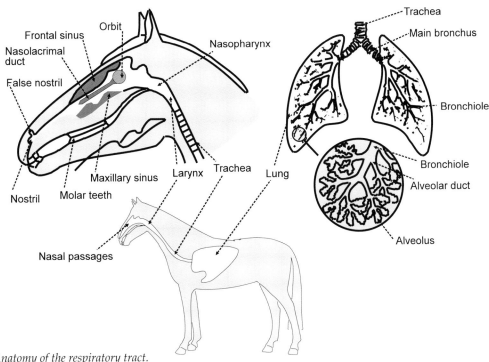

Fig.29. Anatomy of the respiratory tract.

left side of the chest. Each bronchus further divides into progressively smaller branches, the bronchioles, which end at the thin walled alveoli. The alveoli contain cells called macrophages which mop up tiny particles that reach the air sacs, e.g. bacteria and dust. The alveoli are surrounded by a dense network of capillaries. The oxygen in the inhaled air diffuses from the air sacs into the blood stream and is carried mainly in the red blood cells to all tissues of the body. Carbon dioxide diffuses out of the capillaries into the air sacs and is exhaled.

The muscular diaphragm separates the chest from the abdominal cavity. During inspiration the muscles of the diaphragm and those between the ribs (intercostal muscles) contract, causing the chest to expand. Air is drawn into the lungs. When the muscles relax, air is expelled from the lungs and the abdominal muscles assist in pushing air from the lungs. In the healthy resting horse movement of the nostrils, chest wall and abdomen are slight. The respiratory centre in the brain controls the frequency of breathing via the peripheral nerves to the respiratory muscles. The nerve receptors in the blood vessels and the respiratory tract respond to chemical changes. The normal resting rate is 8 to 16 per minute depending on the age and size of animal. At rest the average 500 kg horse takes in 5 lit of air and breathes 12 times per minute.

Management and disease

Respiratory disease is common in equines. The incidence of disease and the type of recovery is greatly influenced by the horse's management system.

Stables should be positioned so that full benefit can be gained from sunlight, making use of windows and skylights where possible to allow sunlight into the building. Ultra-violet light kills many bacteria, viruses and parasites. Stables should be well ventilated without being draughty. Even in well ventilated buildings horses may inhale small fungal spores from contaminated bedding and feed.

The bedding material should be clean and dust free. Straw, however clean, contains more fungal spores than shavings, paper and synthetic bedding material. Deep litter beds should be avoided as mould can easily form and a build-up of bacteria and parasitic larvae will develop. Ammonia in bedding is an irritant to the respiratory tract.

Poorly insulated buildings, especially those with a metal roof can cause condensation and raise humidity. Condensation is also a sign of poor ventilation.

Muck heaps should be positioned well away from stables. Decomposing plant material is a source of mould spores which are easily inhaled. Flies and vermin are attracted to these areas and can spread infections.

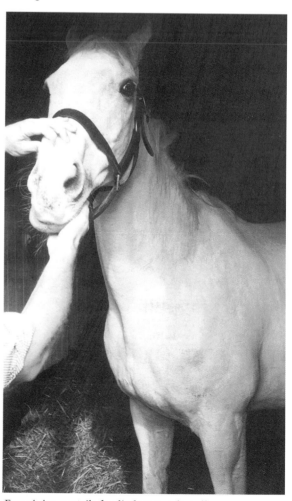

Examining nostrils for discharge and smell

Only good quality, clean forage should be used. Musty or dusty hay will contain millions of spores and is unsuitable for use. Hay barns should be positioned carefully. It is not advisable to store hay in lofts over stables as it is a fire hazard.

Horses need shelter at pasture from driving wind and rain and, depending on climatic conditions, may also need rugs. Animals that are on a poor plane of nutrition or are suffering from other debilitating diseases are more susceptible to respiratory infections. Young animals may have no immunity to certain diseases and are more sensitive to cold. Stress due to overcrowding, hard training and travelling long distances may increase the incidence of disease. The owner can reduce the likelihood of disease by using a high level of care and avoiding conditions that cause poor air quality and contamination of the horse's environment by mould spores.

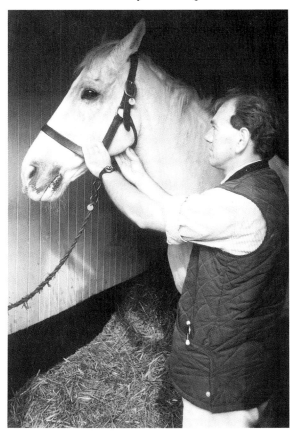
Checking glands and pulse rate

Respiratory disease may affect the upper or lower respiratory tract and be caused by infectious or non-infectious agents. Infections may be viral, bacterial, fungal or parasitic. Allergies, anatomical problems and injuries also cause disease.

Signs of disease

The owner usually notices that the horse's respiratory pattern and rate has altered. There may be exercise intolerance, i.e. unexpected tiredness. There may be a fever, swollen glands, nasal discharge and coughing.

Veterinary assistance is needed if any of the above signs of disease are noticed.

The vet will take a full history of the horse and all the management details before doing a thorough examination. The owner can provide the following information:

Number of animals affected
Age and breed
Stable management
Diet, bedding and grazing routine
Appetite and thirst
Worming and vaccinational history
Exercise routine
Contacts with other equines, e.g. at shows or sales
Duration and signs of illness
Weight loss

The clinical examination will include:

Taking the rectal temperature, pulse and respiratory rate
Observing the depth and type of breathing
Listening to the respiratory tract with a stethoscope
Observing the amount and type of nasal discharge
Palpating the lymph nodes in the throat
The frequency and type of cough e.g., dry or moist, will be noted
Endoscopy of the upper respiratory tract to detect abnormalities.

In order to determine the cause and give the correct medication and an accurate prognosis the vet may need to take samples for laboratory examination.

Blood samples are taken for haematology, to determine the number and types of blood cells

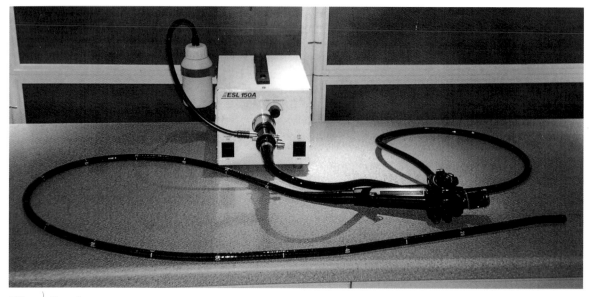

Fibre-optic endoscope

present, and biochemistry and serology to show tissue damage and the presence of antibodies to infectious agents.

Nasal and pharangeal swabs are used to detect and grow organisms on culture plates. Tracheal washes and bronchial/alveolar washes are obtained using an endoscope with a sterile catheter to flush and collect samples. These samples are examined for white blood cells associated with infections and bacteria, fungi and parasites. Faecal samples are used to detect parasites and their eggs. Further techniques involve radiography, diagnostic ultrasound and thermal imaging. .

Viral disease

Many owners refer to any horse showing signs of respiratory disease as having 'the virus' or 'the cough'. In fact many viruses are responsible for these infections, either singly or in combination, e.g.

Equine influenza

This is a highly infectious disease of all equines and is caused by several strains of influenza virus. Both the upper and lower tract are affected and the heart and liver may be inflamed. The incubation period is short, only one to three days so infection can spread rapidly through a susceptible group of animals. Infected animals shed virus for six days. The virus is spread by contact with infected discharges and inhaling droplets propelled into the air by coughing.

The virus causes the following clinical signs:

Depression due to high fever (39° to 40°C [103° to 106°F])
Watery nasal discharge which may become purulent (thick and yellow)
A severe dry harsh cough
Conjunctivitis
Painful glands
Loss of appetite

Secondary bacterial infections of the nose, throat and lungs may complicate the recovery. Chronic obstructive pulmonary disease (COPD), an allergy to fungal spores, may follow a viral infection. The inflamed tissues may be hyper-sensitive to inhaled particles during the course of viral disease which leads to COPD in later life. (See page 55.) The vet should attend any coughing or feverish horse. Clinical signs, nasopharyngeal swabs to isolate the virus and serology to detect antibody levels will confirm a diagnosis.

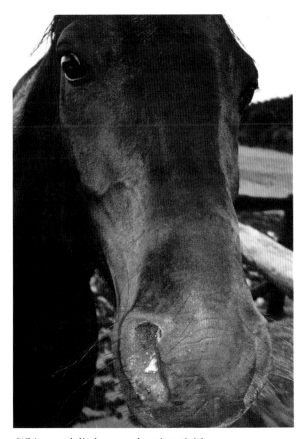

White nasal discharge and conjunctivitis

Treatment involves medication, good nursing and hygiene.

MEDICATION
1 Antibiotics are used to treat secondary bacterial infection.
2 Antipyretics will reduce the fever and improve the appetite.
3 Mucolytics reduce the viscosity of the secretions.
4 Bronchodilators open up the airways and reduce muscle spasm in the walls

NURSING
See page 137.

HYGIENE AND MANAGEMENT
All affected and in contact animals should be isolated and closely monitored.

The horse must stop work and have complete rest for at least a month after all clinical signs have disappeared.

A fresh air regime is important. The horse must be kept in a well ventilated box with minimal access to dust and fungal spores.

PREVENTION
Avoid contact with infected animals and premises with known infections.

Good hygiene and management, i.e. clean stables, bedding and feed. Avoid using other animals' tack and equipment and have individual feeding and watering utensils.

Isolate new horses and those that have travelled long distances or returned from events coughing.

Avoid sharing transport with horses of unknown disease status

Follow a vaccination programme to give the best possible level of immunity to all equines on each premises. (See page 12.)

Equine Herpes Virus 1

There are two forms of this virus; sub-type one EHV 1 and sub-type two also called EHV 4.

EHV 1 can cause abortion in mares, paralysis, respiratory disease and serious disease in new born foals.

EHV 4 mainly causes respiratory disease in young horses. Infection is spread by inhaling virus coughed out from infected animals or from symptomless carriers or from aborted material.

Respiratory signs include:

Upper tract infection
Coughing more common in young animals
Nasal discharge rapidly becoming purulent and may last for three weeks
Fever
Enlarged lymph nodes
Depression and loss of appetite

Diagnosis and treatment of the respiratory forms of the disease are as discussed for equine influenza.

Blood and tissues from aborted or dead foals can be cultured for virus. Horses showing incoordination, dribbling urine or paralysis will need intensive care if they are to recover.

Avoid stress in carrier animals.

All aborting mares and foal deaths must be investigated.

All movement of animals on/off the premises must stop until a diagnosis is made. Presume all in-contact animals are infected.

PREVENTION
Isolation of infected animals and disinfection of the contaminated area.

VACCINATION
See page 12.

Equine Viral Arteritis

This disease was first seen in the U.K. in 1993 and was traced to an imported stallion from Poland. Mares were infected via semen and developed a respiratory disease. EVA infection is spread by contact with any of the body secretions, e.g. urine, faeces, nasal discharge, saliva and milk and aborted foetuses/foetal membranes. Following infection the virus is excreted in all body fluids for up to a month. Stallions may become carriers and shed virus for years in their semen.

The virus can cause:

Fever for many days
Discharge from eyes and nose
Inflamed conjunctiva 'pink eye'
Depression
Swollen legs, head and genitalia
Skin plaques and rashes
Diarrhoea
Coughing
Abortion in mares
Disease in new born foals

There is a Common Code of Practice covering this disease and the importation of horses into the U.K.

Quarantine and blood samples are necessary from horses arriving from EVA infected countries. Horses are blood tested prior to vaccination to see if they have already been infected. Stallions that are free from EVA are vaccinated to prevent them becoming infected and being viral shedders. All suspect cases need veterinary investigation and strict isolation as with EHV 1 abortions.

Bacterial disease

Strangles (Streptococcus equi)

Strangles is a common, highly infectious and contagious disease of all equines, it can occur in any age group but may be more serious in the young, debilitated and elderly animal. Animals develop some immunity after recovery from the disease but many become symptomless carriers and intermittently excrete the bacteria for months. The animal's environment becomes contaminated and handlers can easily spread the infection on hands, clothing and utensils. The incubation period is three to ten days. The clinical signs are those of an upper respiratory tract disease with abscess formation in the lymph nodes and a profuse nasal discharge.

The early signs include:

High fever with depression
Loss of appetite (anorexia) and reluctance to swallow
Watery discharge from nose and eyes
Soft moist cough due to pharyngitis
Slightly swollen glands

Within a few days the signs become more obvious:

Thick copious yellow nasal discharge
Large, painful glands that eventually burst to discharge pus
Difficulty in breathing as the airway is obstructed, often the head and neck are outstretched
Coughing becomes more frequent
Fever persists
Loss of weight

Early treatment is necessary with good nursing care and strict hygiene is needed to avoid spread of infection. Isolation procedures should be carefully followed according to veterinary advice. In contact animals should be closely watched for early signs and their temperatures monitored twice daily.

There may be complications due to abscess formation in lymphoid tissue of internal organs 'bastard strangles'.

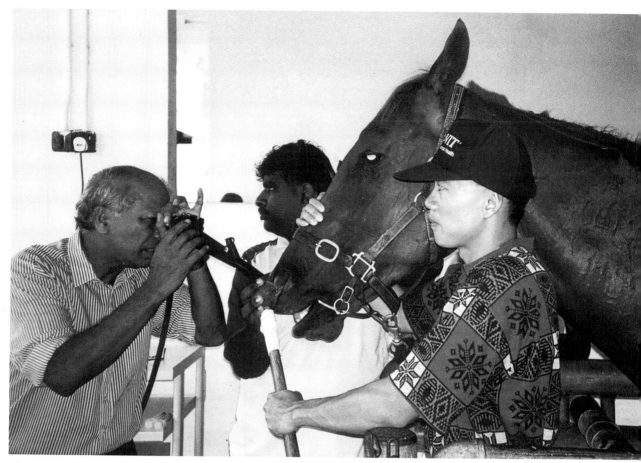

Using an endoscope

Purpura Haemorrhagica can occur one to three weeks after the horse has apparently recovered from strangles. This is an allergic reaction to the bacterial antigens in which the blood vessels are damaged and there is oedema of the limbs, head and ventral body wall. Haemorrhages occur and serum oozes from the skin weals. Intensive nursing and treatment gives only a 50% recovery rate from these complications.

Other bacteria may be involved, both primary and secondary to virus disease of the respiratory tract. They can cause bronchitis, pneumonia and pleurisy. They include: Streptococcus zooepidemicus, Streptococcus pneumoniae, Rhodococcus equi, Bordetella bronchiseptica, Klebsiella sp., Salmonella sp., Pseudomonas sp., E. coli., Pasteurella sp. and various Mycoplasma organisms.

Parasitic disease

Lungworm and roundworm infestation can cause coughing in equines. The diagnosis and treatment is described in Part one, page 17. Animals on the correct management and worming programme should not suffer from these parasite infestations.

Allergic disease

Chronic Obstructive Pulmonary Disease (COPD)

This is a small airway disease of domesticated equines. This allergic disease is also known as emphysema, 'heaves' and 'broken wind'. It may be seen after a viral or bacterial infection and is associated with a hypersensitivity to inhaled airborne dust and fungal spores. The presence of ammonia from urine in stables also damages the airways. Some fungal spores are small enough to avoid being filtered out in the upper airways and reach the small airways where they cause inflammation, excessive mucus production and smooth muscle spasm of the small airway walls. The affected animals show marked respiratory signs at rest; these include a chronic cough, flared nostrils, forced abdominal breathing, increased respiratory rate and depth and some nasal discharge. Advanced or severe cases will be unable to work and show weight loss; milder cases will show variable degrees of exercise intolerance and respiratory distress if worked. The condition is more likely to develop in animals that are not completely rested and allowed to convalesce after an infection. It takes a month for the cilia lining the airways to recover following equine influenza. Animals with a respiratory infection take longer to recover in a dusty environment than in a fresh air regime. Veterinary examina-

tion, early management and treatment may control COPD cases before they become severe. Diagnosis is made on the clinical signs, response to a dust-free environment and therapeutic treatment, endoscopy and examination of tracheal/bronchial washes.

DUST-FREE ENVIRONMENT

This means keeping the horse away from the allergens. If possible the animal should be out at pasture with access to a field shelter. If stabling is necessary, the design and ventilation may need improvement. The main sources of mould spores in the stable are from feed and bedding. The horse should be bedded on shavings, paper or rubber matting. Beds must be cleaned daily and the horse should be removed from the stable area at mucking out time. The stable must be a good distance from the muck heap and straw bedding should not be used in neighbouring stables.

COPD cases should be transported in clean

Using a nebuliser and face mask (C. L. Hocking)

vehicles with no access to hay and straw and should be frequently untied to allow postural drainage of mucus.

Hay of good quality may be fed as long as it is soaked in clean water for up to 30 minutes, drained and fed damp in a container at ground level. Any wet hay landing on the bedding can dry out and the spores will seed the clean bed. The horse will inhale these if it lies down or sniffs the bed. If the hay is allowed to dry out before it is eaten the spores will become airborne again and may be inhaled. Soaking the hay swells the spores and sticks them to the hay. It is important that fresh water is used, otherwise it may ferment. It is not advisable to soak the hay for longer than 30 minutes as this will greatly reduce the nutritional value and turn the soak water into a potent, sewage-like liquid.

There are many alternative forms of forage to hay available for animals with COPD. Haylage; preserved, baled, semi-wilted grasses; treated chaffed hay and straw; complete cubed diets and grass nuts.

Various pharmacological agents are used to alleviate the symptoms of COPD:

1 Mucolytics breakdown secretions and thick mucus blocking airways
2 Bronchodilators open airways, stop broncho-spasm and stimulate mucocilary clearance
3 Antibiotics are required to remove bacterial agents
4 Anti inflammatory agents to reduce acute inflammation
5 Nebulisation with desensitising agents

Nebulisers have been used regularly in humans with asthma and are now used to treat and prevent respiratory disease in horses. The medication is converted into an aerosol of fine droplets which are inhaled using a face mask.

Summer pasture associated obstructive pulmonary disease (SPAOPD)

This condition is seen in horses at pasture without exposure to hay and straw. They show the same clinical signs as COPD cases. They are allergic to a variety of plant pollens and if possible they should be moved to a new location away from blossom and pollen. A fresh air regime and medication to alleviate the symptoms is needed.

Conformation, anatomical problems

Respiratory distress (dyspnoea), exercise intolerance, abnormal respiratory noise during exercise, and difficulty in swallowing and inhalation pneumonia may occur due to abnormalities in the anatomy of the respiratory tract.

Common problems are conditions of the pharynx and larynx, which are diagnosed by endoscopy, e.g.

1 Foals are occasionally born with cleft palates, which require surgical intervention
2 ILH (idiopathic laryngeal hemiplegia). Horses with paralysis of the left vocal chord make a roaring or whistling inspiratory noise at canter or gallop. This condition is normally treated surgically
3 DDSP (dorsal displacement of soft palate). This condition occurs when the soft palate moves over the epiglottis and interferes with airflow during fast work. Gurgling sounds are heard
4 Epiglottic cysts may also cause displacement of the soft palate and the epiglottis.
   Epiglottic entrapment may occur if there is a large fold of mucosal membrane over the epiglottis

Injuries

Accidental injuries may involve and damage any area of the respiratory tract and cause dyspnoea. These injuries are potentially life threatening and require urgent veterinary assistance. Puncture wounds may cause air to leak under the skin or the collapse of a lung. Foreign bodies occasionally block airways and have to be surgically removed. Horses may also suffer from smoke inhalation after stable fires.

THE DIGESTIVE SYSTEM

Anatomy

The digestive tract starts at the mouth and ends at the anus. Horses select their food with their lips, bite off lengths with the incisor teeth and grind it into small 1 mm to 2 mm particles with the cheek teeth (mastication). Dental disease will affect this process.

Saliva is produced when the horse chews and this lubricates the food. It contains bicarbonate ions that buffer the food when it passes into the stomach.

The food bolus, once it is in a suitable form, is moved to the back of the mouth, swallowed and propelled down the muscular oesophagus and into the stomach by waves of peristalsis. This takes 10 to 12 seconds. The oesophagus can be located on the left side of the horse's neck immediately above the trachea in the jugular groove. Inadequately lubricated food can block the oesophagus (see *Choke, page 60*).

The stomach lies in the abdomen against the diaphragm and within the ribcage. The stomach can only hold a small amount, about 2½ kg of food (10 lit). Horses cannot vomit and dilation of the stomach can lead to rupture. The food is mixed with the acidic gastric juices and some protein is broken down. Bacterial fermentation begins in the stomach and the food is physically broken down. The food enters the small intestine and is mixed with the bile and pancreatic juice. The enzymes convert the protein to amino acids and the fats to fatty acids. Some carbohydrates (starch) are converted to simple sugars. Small nutrient molecules are absorbed through the gut wall into the bloodstream. The small intestine is about 21 metres long and food takes less than an hour to pass along it as the smooth muscle walls contract (peristalsis). The digestion of all but insoluble fibre is completed here. Undigested food, mainly fibre enters the large intestine at the ileocaecal junction which is the site where tapeworms attach. The caecum is a large pear-shaped organ on the right side of the abdomen, it is a large fermentation vat containing millions of micro-organisms which break down insoluble

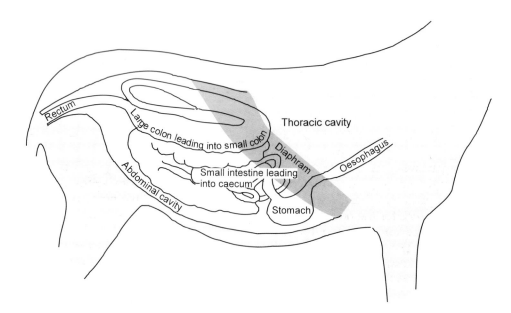

Fig.30. The digestive tract.

Fig.31. The length and capacity of the digestive tract.

Organ	Average length		Average capacity	
	Metric	Imperial	Metric	Imperial
Stomach			10 lts	3 gals
Duodenum	1 metre	3 ft		
Jejunum	20 m	65 ft		
Ileum	1.5 m	4.5 ft		
Caecum	70 cm	2.5 ft	30 lts	7 gals
Large colon	3 - 5 m	12ft	100 lts	22 gals
Small colon	3 - 5 m	12 ft	55 lts	12 gals

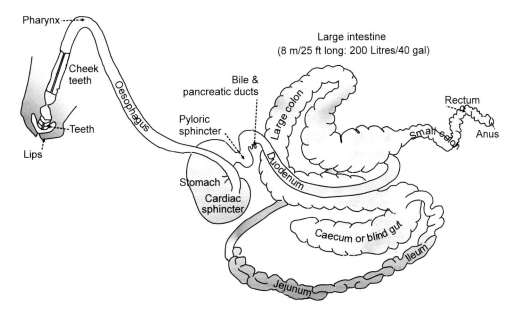

fibre to produce volatile fatty acids (VFAs), and continue the digestion of protein, carbohydrate and fat. These organisms manufacture the B vitamins and vitamin K. The fermentation of fibre is thermogenic, i.e. produces heat, and VFAs provide an energy source for the horse. The caecum opens into the large looped colon where fermentation continues. The food material may remain in the large intestine for two to three days. Water is extracted as the food contents pass along the large bowel. Any dysfunction of the colon, e.g. colitis, will result in diarrhoea. Undigested contents, mainly lignin and waste products, pass into the rectum and are voided as faeces through the anus. Abnormal faeces indicate a bowel disorder.

If the stable bacterial population of the large intestine is disturbed by sudden changes in diet or dietary excesses the horse may develop colic, diarrhoea, azoturia, excitability or laminitis. These are common consequences of overloading the gut with soluble carbohydrates, e.g. spring grass or grain/cereal feed, which pass undigested from the small intestine into the large intestine, where rapid fermentation produces lactic acid.

The friendly bacteria may die due to the alteration in pH of the gut contents. They then release endotoxins that further damage the gut wall, enter the bloodstream, and the resulting toxaemia can kill the horse.

Disorders of the digestive tract

Mouth

Dental disease and the need for regular dental care is discussed in part one, page 22.

Injuries to the incisors, lips and tongue will affect prehension (intake of food). Dysphagia, the inability to eat or swallow may be caused by sharp teeth, mouth ulcers, arthritis of the temporomandibular joint, soft palate abnormalities and paralysis of tongue or pharynx. Neurological conditions which affect swallowing include tetanus, botulism, lead poisoning and grass sickness.

Oesophageal obstruction (Choke)

Choke refers to a blockage in the gullet usually caused by food. This can happen if dry food is bolted, not chewed thoroughly and not lubricated by saliva. Hungry or greedy animals are more likely to bolt their food. Accidentally feeding unsoaked sugar beet cubes is a common cause of choke. Occasionally large pieces of carrots and apples may lodge in the gullet or there may be a narrowing of the oesophagus due to scar tissue or an abscess or tumour. Any reduction in diameter of the oesophagus may predispose to blockage by dry or inadequately chewed food. Obstructions may cause necrosis of the mucosal lining if left for a prolonged time, e.g. 48 hours. This may heal with excessive scarring and narrowing (stricture) of the oesophagus.

Signs of choke are:

Usually a sudden onset after starting a feed
Saliva and food material will drool from the mouth and nostrils
The neck will be alternately extended and arched
The horse may cough and grunt
Dysphagia
Nasal regurgitation of food
Possible inhalation of food and saliva will cause an aspiration pneumonia

Cervical oesophageal obstructions can be seen and palpated over the left jugular groove

All food and water should be removed from the stable and the horse observed for a few minutes. Many cases clear up without veterinary help within 10 minutes.

Animals that do not self cure or are distressed should have veterinary treatment. In the meantime, provide an inedible bed or stay with the horse, prevent it from eating its bed and do not offer any food.

Veterinary treatment includes: sedation, pain relief and muscle relaxation of the oesophageal wall; passing a stomach tube to locate and move

Passing a stomach tube

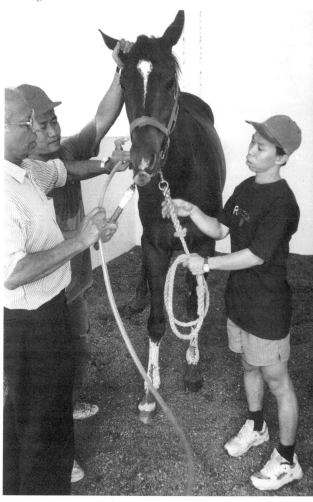

the obstruction by water irrigation down the tube; endoscopy to detect any damage or abnormality.

Most cases recover with conservative treatment within 24 hours but sometimes the obstruction is so firmly impacted that the horse may need to be anaesthetised. The vet will advise on the aftercare.

Obviously after the obstruction has been removed the horse must not be given its usual diet for several days. Grass and small soaked feeds and water may be offered. Wet hay can be introduced after a couple of days if no grazing is available.

It is important to prevent the condition recurring and this may involve changes in management, for example:

Avoid dry cubed feeds
Always offer hay before feeding concentrates
Do not allow animals access to food while they are heavily sedated or recovering from sedation
Avoid peer pressure at feeding times, by feeding separately
Routine dental maintenance

Colic

In the equine world colic simply means abdominal pain. Colic has many different causes and is classified in a variety of ways. Most colics respond to medical treatment but about 10% require prompt surgical intervention if they are

Sugar-beet shreds should be soaked in a jug. Apples and carrots should be chopped into small pieces

to survive. The signs of colic exhibited by the horse depend on the severity of the pain.

Signs of colic are:

Curling upper lip
Flank watching
Restless behaviour as pain increases
Digging and pawing the ground
Repeatedly lying down and rolling
Lying on back
Lying down for long periods
Backing into a corner
Grinding teeth
Sweating
Kicking at abdomen
Straddled position as if to urinate and straining
Anorexia
Alteration in faeces, e.g. constipation or diarrhoea
Flatulence
Elevated pulse and respiratory rate

CAUSES OF COLIC

Parasites
Large redworm, small redworm and tapeworm are all responsible for causing spasmodic colics. They damage the gut mucosa and affect gut motility. Large adult roundworms can block the intestines, especially after worming. Parasite infestation is easy to control by good pasture hygiene and correct use of worming drugs, see page 15.

Environmental factors
Lack of water or inadequate water intake can cause impacted colic as the horse becomes dehydrated. This is exacerbated by hot weather and strenuous exercise and is preventable by allowing free access to water at all times.
Horses grazing on sandy pastures may ingest sand which irritates the gut.
The horse may also eat large amounts of bedding resulting in an impacted colic. This may be avoided by using inedible bedding and providing good quality forage.
Poisonous weeds are usually eaten when grass is in short supply and may cause colic. All poisonous plants should be removed from horse pasture and hay provided there is insufficient grass.

Feeding
High concentrate diets, insufficient forage and sudden changes in diet all have a detrimental effect on the normal bacterial flora of the intestine. Poor quality, spoilt and inappropriate feed such as that intended for sheep, pigs or cattle can cause intestinal upsets. Poor feeding practices such as irregular or over-large meals should be avoided.

Ulcers
Gastric ulceration may cause colicky pain. Ulcers are also associated with colic involving other

Ragwort – a poisonous plant (C. L. Hocking)

parts of the tract. There may be an association between gastric ulcers and intestinal problems.

Enteritis

Infections caused by salmonellosis, intestinal clostridiosis and coccidiosis cause enteritis and colitis. The inflamed gut is painful and the animal will show signs of colic.

Tumours

Tumours of the intestine are not common. They may occasionally cause surgical colics. They are seen in the older equine.

Dental disease

Impactions are common in animals with poor dentition. Regular dental care is important.

Drugs

Several drugs cause bowel dysfunction. Some anti-inflammatory drugs cause gastrointestinal ulceration if used for long periods at high dose rates.

Some sedatives/painkillers used prior to surgery reduce gut motility and in horses that have been starved or are anorexic these may also contribute to post-operative intestinal problems.

Antibiotic therapy, especially the tetracyclines are associated with colitis and diarrhoea as they disturb the gut flora. Horses on oral antibiotics are often given probiotics to help reseed the gut.

Chemical toxins may be inadvertently eaten and cause colic, e.g. arsenic, organophosphorus compounds, monensin.

Other abdominal but non-intestinal causes of colic do occur. The liver, kidneys and reproductive organs are also located inside the abdomen and may be the source of pain. A foaling mare may show colic signs.

Horses with chest pain, e.g. pleuritis, or muscle pain, e.g. azoturia, or acute lameness e.g. laminitis may exhibit some colic-like signs. Frequently the cause of colic is not positively identified or diagnosed but the case responds to symptomatic medical treatment. In surgical cases the reason for a twisted gut is not always obvious.

All cases of colic should be examined by an equine vet. This examination will include:

Taking a detailed case history
Temperature, pulse and respiratory rate
Listening for gut activity
Capillary refill and skin pinch tests
Examination of mucous membranes
Rectal examination

Passing a stomach tube, blood samples and samples of peritoneal fluid may also be required.

Ultrasound may be used, e.g. to detect tumours and X-rays also aid diagnosis, especially in smaller animals including foals.

Colics can be grouped into medical or surgical colics. Medical colics are amenable to medical treatment. After a thorough examination of the horse, the vet will select the appropriate medication for that animal. Treatment is tailored to each case. Types of medical colic are:

Spasmodic colic
This is the commonest form of colic, about 70% are in this group. The normal regular peristalsis is disrupted. The movement becomes irregular and violent. Parasites and feeding problems are often the underlying cause.

Listening to gut sounds

The horse shows pain relating to gut spasms interspersed with normal behaviour.

These cases respond to antispasmodic medicines and analgesia (pain relief)

Tympanitic/flatulent colic

This is caused by gas distending the gut due to over fermentation of unsuitable food, usually grass cuttings, fruit or clover. This problem may resolve untreated or the gut may need to be decompressed. Analgesia is often required together with anti-fermentative drugs. Gas-filled portions of gut may float out of their normal position.

Impactions of the large intestine

This is usually caused by dry and coarse food material completely or partially blocking the gut lumen. Affected animals usually have a history of dental problems, water shortage, unsuitable diet and irregular exercise. The common sites this occurs in are those where there is a sudden reduction in diameter of the gut, such as at the pelvic flexure of the left colon and at the junction of the large and small colon.

This usually is treated with fluids and lubricants given by stomach tube. Colic drinks/drenches should not be used on equines. Large volumes of fluid can only be given safely by stomach tube. The ingredients in colic drenches are not suitable for all types of colic and may be harmful.

Gastric and small intestinal impactions require prompt surgery.

Surgical colic

These are either simple cases where the bowel is obstructed without compromising the blood supply or complex ones where the bowel is twisted or strangulated and the blood supply is cut off. In the first condition the displaced bowel has to be returned to its normal position. The horse will be in pain and shocked but not suffering from toxaemia. When the blood supply has been obstructed the section of dead bowel is resected and the healthy tissue on either side joined up. These animals rapidly develop endotoxic shock as the dead bowel wall leaks its contents into the peritoneum.

Colic surgery

This is a specialised procedure and is performed in an equine operating theatre by a team of surgeons, nurses and an anaesthetist. The horse will require specialised post-operative nursing with careful monitoring and fluid therapy.

If the equine hospital is a long distance away or the animal is unlikely to survive the journey or the case is inoperable the only alternative is humane euthanasia. It is wise to insure all equines for veterinary fees as colic surgery is expensive. Horses that receive prompt veterinary attention,

an early diagnosis and specialist care are likely to make a good recovery from surgery. Some surgical teams hope for a 70 to 80% success rate and full return to athletic work.

What the owner can do while waiting for the vet to arrive

It is important that no one is injured, so great care must be taken in handling a horse that is in pain. Animals that are lying quietly should be observed from a distance. Buckets and mangers should be removed in case the horse rolls. It is safer to leave animals that are rolling violently in a flat field or menage, rather than in a stable where they may injure themselves. Traditionally all colic cases were prevented from rolling as this was thought to twist the guts but it is now accepted that normal horses roll without such a mishap. Horses may injure their head or limbs or may become cast when rolling repeatedly. Colicky animals used to be force walked for hours, this is harmful as it tires the animal who may actually be more comfortable lying down.

Animals with colic should not be offered food or water before they have been assessed by the vet. Colic drenches should not be given.

The owner could monitor pulse and respiratory rate, gut sounds, the passing of urine/faeces, flatulence, colour of mucous membranes and capillary refill at regular intervals, if the horse is calm. This information will be useful for the vet.

Movement of other horses and people should be kept to a minimum as this may disturb the patient.

Grass sickness

Grass sickness or equine dysautonomia has killed hundreds of equines since 1909 when it was first described. The causal agent has not been isolated despite extensive scientific research, but a fungal toxin is thought to be the possible agent. In this condition the digestive tract is paralysed as the autonomic nerve supply degenerates.

Grass sickness can affect any breed of horse, pony or donkey. It occurs in mares, geldings and stallions. Animals in the two to seven year age range are more commonly affected.

The disease is most frequently seen between April and July and often follows a week or more of cool and dry weather.

Most cases occur in grazing animals. Frequently the animal has grazed on the same pasture for less than two months. Certain fields are known to have a high incidence of grass sickness cases. Stress, surgery, travel and mixing with new animals on a new premises may be predisposing factors to this disease. These are common factors in the clinical history notes.

Depending on the degree of gut paralysis, grass sickness may be an acute, a sub-acute or a chronic disease.

Acute cases have a high pulse rate, sweat, muscle tremors and severe colic with a distended abdomen. They salivate and often stomach contents reflux down their nostrils. They are constipated and pass small amounts of hard faecal pellets. They die within two days so these cases should be euthanased as soon as possible.

Sub-acute cases survive for two to seven days. They have a mild to moderate colic with patchy sweating, muscle tremors, dysphagia and obvious weight loss. Those that do not die progress to the chronic stage.

Chronic grass sickness cases have varying difficulty in swallowing both food and water. They chew slowly and pouch food in the mouth, often quidding. They 'fake' drinking, playing with water, so froth is seen on the water and over buckets and the surrounding area. They have mild episodes of colic.

The nostrils become dry and crusty and the eye lids droop. These animals are depressed, have a poor appetite and rapid weight loss. They look 'tucked up' with a greyhound shape to their abdomen.

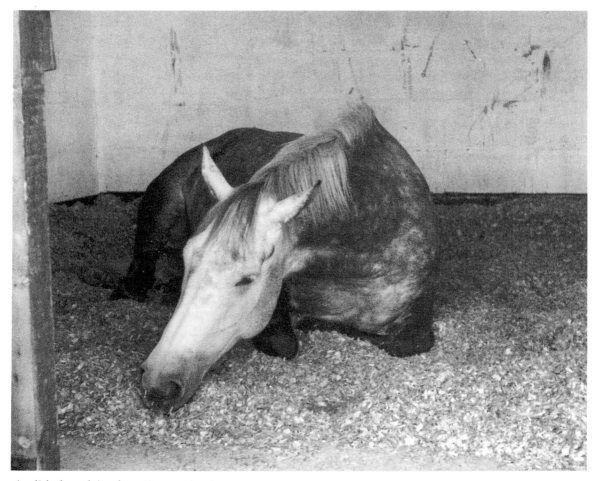

A colicky horse lying down (C. L. Hocking)

The diagnosis is difficult as other causes of colic appear clinically similar. Thorough examination and specific blood tests are needed to make a diagnosis.

Histological examination of gut biopsy samples taken from the ileum (area of small intestine) is a reliable confirmatory test. In grass sickness the damaged nerve cells are detected in strained microscopic sections using an electron microscope.

TREATMENT

A small number of chronic cases will respond to treatment. Careful screening and selection of cases is mandatory. Animals must be able to swallow soft food and drink and have enough body fat to survive for the first two to three weeks with a poor appetite. They should still have an interest in life. Animals that fill this criteria will then require intensive nursing by experienced staff. Recovery is slow in cases that respond to treatment. Cisaprid is used eight hourly to stimulate gut activity. Major setbacks like pneumonia, choke and colic episodes may occur at any time. Inhalation pneumonia is an early complication. About 50% of chronic cases recover but may still experience sweating and changes in their coat. Care in feeding is needed to prevent choke. These animals should be kept stress free and not over exercised. They can be ridden once they return to the correct body weight. See nursing pages 138–9.

PREVENTION

Until the causal agent is found it is not possible to prevent grass sickness. It is advisable not to graze animals on high risk pasture land. Avoid grazing after periods of dry cool weather, especially from April to July. Try to make moves to new premises stress free.

The Skin

Anatomy

The skin or integument is the largest organ of the body, covering the entire body surface. It varies in thickness from 1 to 6 mm. Areas liable to greater wear and tear have thicker skin. The condition of the skin and coat is a good indicator of the health, level of hydration and nutritional status of the horse (see skin pinch test and condition scoring pages 8, 118). The surface layer, the epidermis covers the deeper dermis which lies over the subcutaneous fascia, a loose connective tissue containing nerves and blood vessels. The skin has many important functions. It is a protective barrier to physical injury and infective agents and prevents water and salt loss. It relays information from the animal's environment by sensory nerve receptors that detect changes in temperature, pressure, touch and pain. It synthesises vitamin D when exposed to sunlight and acts as a storage organ for fat and water. It is part of the body's thermoregulatory system, e.g. secretion of sweat to lose heat; erection of hair to conserve heat. The pigment in skin protects the tissues from harmful sun rays. It produces specialised structures such as hoof horn, chestnuts, ergots and hair.

The epidermis has a hard, keratinised waterproof surface made up of tightly bonded cells which are constantly worn away to be replaced by the next layer of cells. The base layer of the epidermis produces new cells which take about two weeks to migrate to the surface. The epidermis also contains the pigment producing cells, the melanocytes.

The dermis consists of a protein matrix with elastin and collagen fibres to give strength and pliability to the skin. It has an intricate blood and nerve supply and also contains hair follicles, sweat and sebaceous glands. The hair follicles and sweat glands are formed by invaginations of the epidermis. Each hair follicle produces a single hair, which grows at an angle to the skin surface so the hair normally lies flat. Hair is continually falling out and being replaced by a new hair that goes through a growing stage followed

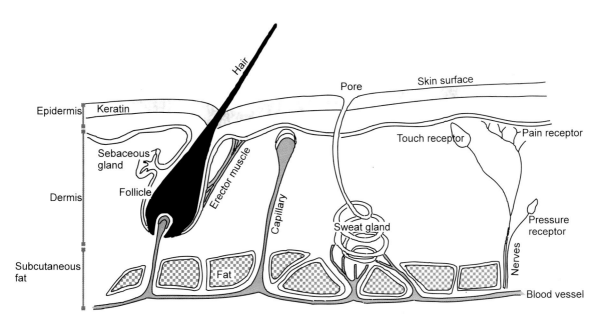

Fig.32. The structure of the skin.

by a resting stage. Hair protects the skin and provides insulation.

Whorls are a hair pattern created by follicles being at different angles. They are used on diagrams as part of the identification of the horse along with colour and non-pigmented hair, skin and hoof wall. Hair colour is inherited and genetically controlled. Acquired marks are areas of white hair resulting from skin damage, such as saddle sores, boot or bandage rubs and girth galls. Unpigmented skin is more susceptible to sunburn, and cream hooves are thought to be weaker than black hooves.

The shedding of the coat is under environmental and hormonal control in the spring and autumn, when the thick, winter coat is replaced by a fine, summer coat and vice versa. The mane and tail hairs are coarser, permanent hairs. There are long, tactile hairs around the muzzle and finer hairs on the teats and inside the ears. Eyelashes are specialised hairs.

The sebaceous gland secretes sebum onto the hair to make it pliable and acts as a waterproofing agent. Sebaceous glands produce the waxy surface on the udder, sheath and around the anus and dock. The muscle attached to the hair erects the hair when the horse is cold which helps to empty the sebaceous gland.

Sweat glands open onto the skin surface where sweat evaporates causing heat loss. They are found in most areas of the horse's skin. The greatest numbers are on the flank, the mammary gland and beside the nostrils. They are essential for electrolyte balance, excretion of waste products and temperature control.

Management

Normally horses keep their skin and coat in good condition by self-grooming, e.g. rolling, shaking, licking, nibbling, scratching and rubbing. They also perform mutual grooming with a close companion.

Domestication can make self-grooming difficult for the horse. Stables may be too small for the horse to roll safely and it may roll on faeces which it would normally avoid. Rugs, boots and hoods make it impossible for the horse to groom itself. They also prevent the synthesis of vitamin D. Horses that are tied up are unable to reach most of their body with their mouths, so cannot lick or nibble those areas. Animals with neck pain, lameness and those that are ill often stop self-grooming so their coats soon look neglected.

Grooming

Horses should be groomed every day in a manner to suit their management system. This means that the horse is handled regularly, whether it is in work or not. Grooming should be a pleasant experience for the animal if done in the correct way. Heavy handed grooming or using hard brushes on sensitive areas will upset the horse. Grooming stimulates the circulation, disperses sebum from the sebaceous glands and massages the skin and underlying muscle masses such as the hindquarters. Cleaning the eyes, nose and dock are included in the grooming process. The udder or sheath may need washing with separate sponges used for each area. The feet should be picked out as part of this routine.

The grooming equipment needs regular cleaning as do rugs, boots clippers, tack etc. Detergents should not be used on horse clothing. There are a number of bactericidal and fungicidal shampoos which can be used on both the horse and its equipment. The owner can check the horse for signs of injury and skin disease while grooming.

Signs of skin disease are:

Behavioural signs of irritation, e.g. excessive rubbing/scratching
Restless, stamping feet, tail swishing, head tossing. There may be self-inflicted injuries
Broken hair, dull, staring coat, scurf
Bald areas
Abnormal amount of hair, e.g. long, curly coat
Failure to sweat or excessive sweating
Inflamed skin, scabs, pustules, open wounds, ulcers
Abnormal swelling, e.g. skin wheals, areas of thickened skin, abscesses and tumours
Alteration in skin pigment
Presence of parasites, e.g. lice, ticks, mites, bot eggs.

Housing and shelter

Shelter should be available to protect the horse from inclement weather and strong sunlight as well as nuisance insects. Animals with unpigmented muzzles are prone to sunburn and may also require the added protection of a high factor sunscreen. Wet weather can also cause rain scald and mud rash. These can be prevented by providing a field shelter with a hard standing, by using waterproof rugs and avoiding turn-out pastures which are poorly drained. Muddy, poached areas of fields can be electric fenced to allow the ground to recover.

Clipping

Animals who fail to shed their coat (Cushing's disease) should be clipped out, otherwise they

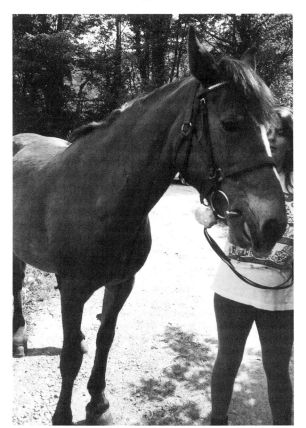

Swelling caused by a fly bite at the base of the neck

become sweaty, uncomfortable and prone to skin infections.

Animals in regular hard work may also require clipping, to prevent heat stress and allow them to dry quickly after work. There is no point in clipping a horse just to be fashionable. Electrical clippers should be quiet, have sharp blades and be properly cleaned, well maintained and used by a competent person. Battery operated and mechanical hand clippers are suitable for small areas and on horses that are nervous of electrical clippers. Some horses require sedation by the vet before clipping. Animals that are clipped should be provided with correctly fitting rugs in the stable and at pasture.

Each animal should have its own equipment, i.e. rugs, tack and grooming kit to avoid inadvertently transmitting skin diseases to other equines.

Fly problems

Flies are a seasonal problem and many species can cause problems to the horse and rider. House flies annoy the animal by swarming around its head and feeding on the discharges from the eyes, nostrils and sheath. They are attracted to wounds where they spread infection.

The Habronema larvae cause summer sores. Sores near the eyes can cause conjunctivitis as the animal rubs its face to remove the insects. Older and long-coated geldings seem to attract flies around their sheaths. Urine splashes onto the hair in front of the sheath. Geldings should have their sheaths cleaned to remove discharges which are attractive to flies. The hair should be clipped from the abdomen in front of the sheath.

Flies cause inflammation of sensitive skin and serum oozing from the wounds attracts more flies. Wounds in summer time can quickly become infested with maggots (myiasis or fly strike). This is why routine surgical procedures like castrations are avoided in the summer. Accidental wounds should be covered with a dressing whenever possible, or a wound ointment, which will repel/kill insects, may be used on the skin surrounding the injury.

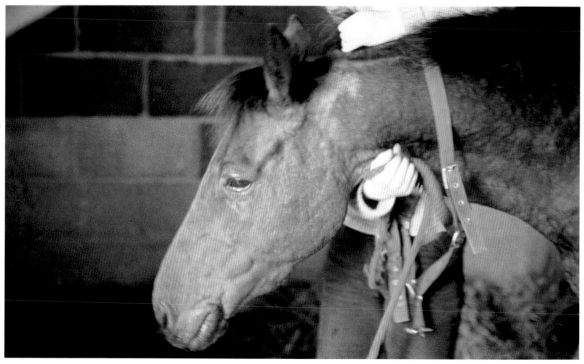

Urticaria (C. L. Hocking)

Stable and horse flies give painful bites which distress the horse and can make it difficult to control. The horse may accidentally kick the handler when it is bitten. Large painful swellings may appear at the site of the bite. Swellings in areas where tack is placed may prevent the animal being ridden under saddle for a few days. Horses may be allergic to the bites of certain insects, and produce very large swellings which require treatment. Some develop hard nodular swellings that remain for months as a reaction to the original bite.

Many horses, ponies and donkeys have an allergy to midge bites, this is called Sweet itch. The bite of the Culicoides midge is painful and the saliva causes a hypersensitivity in some animals. This causes intense irritation and the animal rubs itself raw if left unprotected.

Fly control

There are a variety of methods used to control and reduce the fly problem. It is best to start a control programme early in the spring. In order to breed the insects need warm, moist conditions where there is a plentiful supply of food. Flies congregate around manure heaps so these should be sited away from animal housing and removed weekly. Stable hygiene is important and deep litter beds must be avoided. Pools of urine and water should not be allowed to gather in front of shelters and stables.

Chemical protection

It is important to use fly repellents and/or insecticides before the horse is bitten. Insecticides kill adult flies and can be used on stable walls, manure heaps and applied to the horse's coat. Fly papers and insecticide blocks can be hung from the ceiling. All insecticides should be used according to the manufacturer's instructions. Horses that are frequently bathed or washed after exercise will need insecticide chemicals reapplied. The oily permethrin pour-on products are spread over the body on the grease on the skin and usually last for two to four weeks, providing they are not washed off. Permethrins also kill lice, forage and harvest mites. Fly repellents do not kill flies but deter them from landing on the horse. They are usually only effective for a few hours and then have to be reapplied. Some contain natural oils like citronella. Repellents are applied prior to riding the horse so the animal is not constantly annoyed by flies. The flies can continue to breed and multiply if only repellents are used. Whenever a new product is used on the horse it is important to do a test spot first, on a small area of skin to make sure that there will be no adverse reaction. The manufacturer's instructions should be carefully followed and any adverse reaction reported to the veterinary supplier. Adding garlic to the horse's feed is supposed to help keep flies away, although this has not been scientifically proven.

Physical protection

Horses can be stabled during the day, when the flies are most active. Fly fringes, veils and hoods must be used with care and the horse closely supervised. Lightweight summer sheets will keep the flies off the horse while in the stable, field and when travelling. Well sited field shelters positioned away from trees, water and manure heaps provide a cool, shady place away from the flies during hot weather.

No one method will totally control flies; it is necessary to use good management combined with repellents and insecticides.

Parasitic skin diseases

Lice

Equines may be infested by biting lice, Damalinia equi, which feed on scurf and skin debris or by sucking lice, Haematopinus asini, which feed on blood and tissue fluid. Lice are a seasonal problem seen in mid to late winter when animals have long coats. Both lice and their eggs (nits) are visible to the naked eye, adult lice are grey, about 3 mm long and live on the host. They lay cream-coloured nits onto the base of hairs, especially the mane and forelock. The life-cycle takes two to three weeks.

Louse infestation is transmitted by direct contact with infested animals, their grooming equipment, tack and rugs. Debilitated animals and those suffering from immune suppressive disorders, e.g. Cushing's disease, may be severely affected.

Signs of infestation are easy to detect. Lice cause irritation and rubbing, so the animal's coat has a moth-eaten appearance with bald patches and broken hairs. Some animals are very sensitive to lice infestation and do not need to harbour large numbers of the parasite before they show pruritis. The head, neck, flanks and croup are usually affected. Severe cases will lose condition and become anaemic.

Animals can be treated with permethrin preparations at two weekly intervals to kill newly hatched lice. All in-contact animals and equipment must be treated at the same time. The ivermectin wormer medicines may help to control lice as these chemicals circulate in the blood to the skin.

Harvest mites (Trombicula) and forage mites (Acarus spp)

Both harvest and forage mites can produce skin disease in equines. The adult and nymph stages of these parasites are free living (non-parasitic), it is only the larval stage that feeds on mammals. The more usual host is a small rodent, but they may parasitise horses. Animals at pasture are infested in late summer and autumn by larvae of harvest mites; the limbs, head and trunk being commonly affected. They cause small papules with hair loss and intense irritation. Preserved hay and bedding straw may harbour numerous forage mites that induce disease at any time of the year in the stabled animal.

Mite infestations also cause intense pruritus in some individuals and, like lice, can be treated with pour-on permethrin preparations.

The infested straw and forage should be removed from the patient's environment and preferably burned.

Mange mites

Chorioptic mange is seen on the lower limbs of heavy horses and those with 'feather', especially in winter. The mite has a two to three week life-cycle and is able to live off the host for a couple of days. The mite burrows into the skin of the cannon, fetlock and pastern causing pruritus, leg stamping and self mutilation. There is usually scab formation and scaly skin. Neglected cases may result in Greasy heel, a form of dermatitis that is difficult to treat. Diagnosis is made on clinical signs and skin scrapings from the affected areas should contain parasites which can be identified under the microscope. Treatment involves removing all the feather (leg hair) and applying ectoparasiticides.

Psoroptic mange is seen on the head, ears, mane and tail. It causes pruritus and head shaking. Papules, moist scabs and bald areas are commonly seen.

The mite can live off the host for a couple of weeks on grooming utensils etc.

A diagnosis is made on examining skin scrapings.

Treatment involves clipping and cleaning the affected areas and using ectoparasiticides. Headcollars and other equipment should be thoroughly cleaned.

Ticks

These are blood sucking parasites and can transmit diseases from one host to another, e.g. Lyme's disease.

In the U.K. sheep ticks can parasitise equines. They are found in heathland and bracken areas. Ticks are large, round and usually seen in groups on the horse's abdomen. Ticks are firmly attached to the skin while they are feeding and are difficult to remove without leaving their mouthparts in situ. They can be killed by applying an acaricide directly on to the tick.

PREVENTION
Keep equines off tick infested land. Sheep that are dipped after shearing and in the late summer are less likely to carry ticks. Bracken should be removed from grazing areas as it is poisonous to livestock and carcinogenic.

Oxyuris (Pinworm)

The adult pinworm lays its eggs on the perineum of the horse causing anal irritation and tail rubbing.

DIAGNOSIS
The eggs can be removed on clear sticky tape and identified microscopically.

TREATMENT
Wash perineum and treat skin lesions as wounds. Use any anthelmintic preparation as advised.

Stables and fittings should be periodically steam cleaned.

Fungal disease

Ringworm

Ringworm is the commonest fungal infection seen in equines. It is highly contagious and spreads easily in four to seven days in humid conditions and four to five weeks in a dry, cold winter. There are a number of fungal species that can infect horses and also humans. Care should be taken when handling and treating ringworm patients! Although the condition is not serious it is unsightly, expensive and time consuming to treat. Once a premises has become infected it is difficult to eliminate the ringworm spores. The spores are resistant to most environmental conditions and disinfectants and can survive for years on wooden fences and in buildings.

Trichophyton and Microsporum species are usually responsible for equine ringworm. Other species not specific to horses can spread to other animals e.g. cattle, dogs and cats.

Ringworm is seen in areas where there is friction or abrasions, so under tack and boots are a common site for lesions, e.g. saddle, girth, martingale. Riders' boots can spread infections from one horse to another. Ringworm is more common in winter time, which may be due to spread by clipping and hard grooming to remove mud. The active spores will penetrate abraded skin. In winter horses tend to be stabled and kept in closer proximity to each other and possible infection.

SIGNS OF RINGWORM

Unfortunately the skin lesions are variable in appearance and may be confused with other skin diseases. Some cases show spherical areas of dry, scaly skin and hair loss, while others form a crusty scab around tufts of hair. The horse soon develops more lesions and the original area may become a large irregular shaped patch. The lesions may appear anywhere on the body and only cause mild irritation. If left untreated the signs usually disappear in eight to twelve weeks but by then the highly resistant spores will be widely disseminated and many animals may be affected. Whole yards may be involved in an outbreak.

DIAGNOSIS AND TREATMENT

If ringworm is suspected it is important to have an early diagnosis and prompt treatment to prevent contamination of the horse's environment and infection spreading to other animals.

The diagnosis is made on the clinical signs and the history of other infected animals. Skin, hair and scabs are examined microscopically for fungal spores and hyphae. The fungi can also be cultured on special media plates in an incubator which may take a couple of weeks.

The horse is usually given in-feed medication and antifungal/sporicidal washes at three to five day intervals. The horse's environment and all equipment also has to be cleaned with a sporicidal/fungicidal disinfectant. Woodwork can then be creosoted. Strict hygiene measures are necessary to avoid infection of handlers and other horses. The handler should wear overalls to prevent contaminating their clothes.

All at-risk animals should be carefully inspected each day for a couple of weeks after the last new case. Avoid grooming or clipping the horse as this spreads the spores. An easily cleaned cotton sheet may be used under a rug to avoid having to repeatedly wash thick rugs. Horses with ringworm obviously should be isolated and not

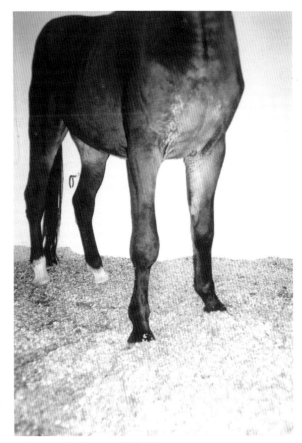

Ringworm lesions on the brisket

travelled or competed. If the lesions are under the saddle or girth the horse should not be exercised under saddle.

The treatment involves care of the patient and care of the equipment and stable which is very time consuming. The horse will be resistant to that species of ringworm for six to twelve months.

Bacterial skin diseases

A number of bacteria found on the skin surface and in the horse's environment may cause inflammation of the skin (dermatitis), or the hair follicles (folliculitis) or the dermis, (furunculosis), (acne). If the skin surface is injured, the resulting wound allows bacteria to enter the tissues to form an abscess or cellulitis.

Dermatophilosis

The commonest cause of dermatitis is Dermatophilus congolensis. This bacterium causes mud rash and rainscald in areas of skin that are continually wet. The skin feels lumpy with the hair matted into typical paintbrush lesions. Attached to the hair tufts are scabs that are moist on the skin surface. The skin is usually inflamed and may be painful. The skin over the pasterns may crack and ooze serum. Mud rash affects the lower limbs while rainscald is seen on the neck, back and rump. It is usually seen in mild, wet winters but can occur at other times of the year when the ground or pasture is wet. The organism penetrates skin that is damaged and then softened by wet conditions. Animals with thick coats and feathered legs are more prone to mud fever as they take longer to dry than fine coated animals.

Secondary bacterial infection with Staphylococcal spp may complicate mud rash and these cases will require swabs and samples to be taken to establish the cause. The horse may become systemically sick with fever and swollen lymph nodes. These animals will resent their legs being handled and be lame. Treatment of the milder cases involves clipping the hair and using antibacterial washes on the affected skin. This must be thoroughly dried and antibiotic cream applied. It is important not to use strong antiseptics or shampoos as these will inflame the skin and make the condition worse.

The horse must be kept dry so in most cases this means stabling. The bedding should be clean and dry and the legs bandaged using a non-adherent dressing, gamgee and wool stable bandages. This will prevent bedding from sticking to and abrading the damaged areas. If the horse is not lame it may be exercised on dry roads or tracks. If possible the horse can be tied up on the yard or placed in an empty stable, so the legs may be left uncovered for a short time each day. Severe cases may require antibiotics given systemically as well as pain relief. Lame animals should not be ridden.

Mud rash may be prevented by carefully inspecting the horse's legs each day and avoiding excessive wetting of the skin. Hairy legs need clipping so that they dry more easily. Muddy legs should be allowed to dry and then the mud brushed off with a soft body brush. The legs should not be hosed as this does not remove all the mud and makes the legs very wet. They can be properly washed to remove all traces of mud and then thoroughly dried. Wool leg wraps or Thermatex wraps which wick moisture to the surface may be used, or alternatively a hairdrier on a cool setting. Avoid using muddy areas in the winter and provide a hard standing in the field shelter. Remember to clean all the grooming equipment and boots frequently.

Rainscald will normally resolve if the horse's skin is kept dry. The horse should be stabled, the scabs gently removed and the area washed with a mild antibacterial solution and dried. Once the condition has resolved the horse should be provided with a waterproof rug and shelter from wet weather.

Cotton sheets are easy to wash and may be placed under all other rugs. With good hygiene and stable management these conditions are usually preventable.

Skin tumours

Skin tumours are the most common type of tumour seen in horses. They can be benign like the lipoma and fibroma or malignant like squamous cell carcinoma and melanoma. It is important that all tumours are properly investigated using biopsy techniques with laboratory diagnosis. A prognosis is then made depending on the type of tumour, its position and growth rate.

The most common skin tumour is the equine sarcoid. This is thought to be caused by a virus. There are six types of sarcoid seen in horses. These are found on the inner thigh, sheath or udder, neck, head, elbow and girth areas. They are commonly seen on the ventral body wall. Types of sarcoid are:

1 Occult sarcoid. Circular grey scaly patches
2 Verrucous sarcoid. Crusty, wart-like irregular shaped growths
3 Nodular sarcoid. Smooth, nodular swelling under normal looking skin

require early treatment. The options available are:

1 Surgical removal
2 Radiation therapy
3 BCG vaccine
4 Cryosurgery
5 Topical chemotherapy
6 Implants and injections into the tumour with cytotoxic chemical

Sarcoids are a serious disorder and need to be diagnosed early if treatment is to be effective.

Allergic skin diseases

The most common skin allergy in equines is Sweet itch. This is due to a hypersensitivity to the bites of midges (Culicoides). Other insects such as the black fly (Simulium) occasionally cause a similar condition. Animals may also develop a skin reaction to food allergies, contact allergies or skin parasites including pinworm infestation.

Although Sweet itch is seen in all types and breeds of horse and pony it is more common in certain breeds, e.g. the Welsh pony and shire-horse which suggests that there is a genetic influence. It is not sensible to breed from animals with Sweet itch. It is not normally seen in animals under two years of age. Affected animals react to the midge bites by rubbing at the bitten areas, causing open wounds and further problems from other insects attracted to the wounds.

The culicoid midges are blood sucking; their bites are painful and annoy the animal, causing intense irritation. Depending on the species of midge, the horse may be bitten on the head, neck, back or ventral midline. Animals who show an allergic reaction to the bites gradually over the years develop grossly thickened skin and hairloss in the affected areas. These animals are very distressed and spend hours rubbing and scratching.

The midges are most active at dawn and dusk. They like warm and moist conditions and congregate around muck heaps, under trees and near open water. They do not like exposed and windy conditions. Sweet itch is a seasonal

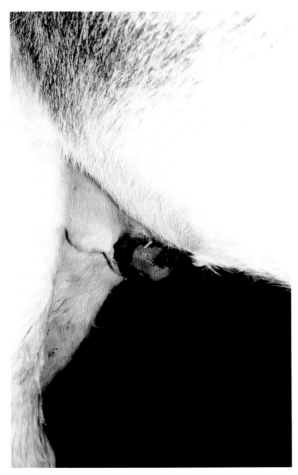

A tumour on the prepuce

4 Fibroblastic sarcoid. Very aggressive mass often ulcerated. May complicate skin wounds
5 Malevolent sarcoid. Invasive tumour which infiltrates the lymphatic system
6 Mixed sarcoid. Contains a mix of the other types

Affected animals usually have multiple tumours of various sizes. They are thought to be spread by biting flies and may spread to other in-contact equines. They can spread locally and be difficult to treat. They often recur at the original site or develop at a new site, making treatment expensive and time consuming. Animals with only a few small tumours that are not likely to be rubbed by tack or rugs may not require treatment, only close observation after initial veterinary diagnosis. Severe cases are not treatable. Tumours that fall between these two groups may

insecticidal sprays can be used as previously described. (See page 70.) No one preparation can be expected to protect a highly sensitised animal unless there are management controls. At present there is no cure and no single effective form of prevention.

Photosensitivity

Horses at pasture can develop sunburn-like lesions due to photosensitivity caused by eating certain plants, e.g. St John's Wort. These plants contain photodynamic chemicals which are absorbed from the gut into the blood. On reaching areas of unpigmented skin they react with sunlight and cause blistering of the skin. This is painful and may become infected by

A sign of Sweet itch – a badly rubbed tail

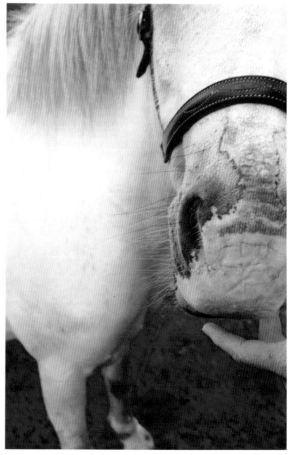

Signs of photosensitivity

condition seen from spring to autumn but if the climate continues to change we may see midges in the winter months. Good management is the key to success with this condition. It is important to identify the early signs to prevent unnecessary suffering.

Treatment with antihistamines or corticosteroids is not usually successful and cannot be used in the long-term. Long-acting steroids may precipitate acute laminitis.

The sensitised animal must be kept away from the midges and every effort should be made to achieve this. The horse should have an insect-proof stable and a protective rug with a hood. The horse can be stabled at times when the midges are most active. Fly repellents are useful in combination with housing the horse and

bacteria. The areas must be kept clean by careful bathing and covered in an antibiotic cream. Lesions on the muzzle and lips will make eating difficult. Forage may be damped and fed from a shallow bowl rather than a net or rack.

These animals have to be housed during daylight and not allowed to graze on pasture where these plants grow.

Photosensitisation is also a symptom of liver disease.

Phylloerythrin, a light sensitive chemical, accumulates in the skin of animals with liver dysfunction. This is a normal product of plant digestion which is normally removed from the circulation by the liver and excreted in the bile. Blood tests are needed to diagnose liver disease. Ragwort poisoning is a common cause of chronic liver damage.

For prevention of sunburn see page 69.

Sores and galls

Saddle sores, girth galls and pressure sores all result from friction and abnormal pressure on areas of skin. They are a result of poor stable management and are caused by tack, rugs, bandages and insufficient bedding.

Saddle sores are seen on the horse's back as

Sunburn around the eyes

Girth gall

raised areas of skin, painful to touch and usually covered with broken hairs. Sites of old sores will have white hair (acquired marks). They are caused by poorly fitting saddles, bad riding, dirty saddles and numnahs, incorrectly positioned rollers and surcingles.

Saddle sores must be allowed to heal completely before the horse can be ridden again. The tack should be cleaned and saddles inspected by a saddler to prevent further problems.

Girth galls are injuries to the girth area and have similar causes to saddle sores. They are prevented by keeping girths clean and using a protective sleeve over the girth. It is important to check the girth is not too loose or too tight as both situations will damage the skin.

Pressure sores are commonly seen over bony prominences in recumbent animals and under incorrectly applied bandages. Animals that are stabled need sufficient bedding to prevent injury being caused by contact with hard floors.

All these conditions should be treated as wounds. (See page 126.)

THE EYE

Anatomy

The horse's eyes are positioned on the side of its head, which gives good all-round vision except for the area directly behind its quarters. The eyeball is slightly flattened so both near and far images can be in focus at the same time. The horse has to move its head up or down to focus clearly on a particular image.

The eye consists of the eyeball, the eyelids and the muscles to move the eye.

The lacrimal apparatus produces tears which coat the surface of the eye. The tears drain through a series of ducts which join together and open onto the floor of each nostril at the junction of the skin and the pink mucous membrane inside the nose. Tears can be seen running from the nostrils. If the ducts are blocked or the horse is producing an excessive volume of tears they will overflow down the face. Tears kill bacteria and wash away debris. The horse has both upper and lower eyelids covered by the conjunctiva on the inside and skin on the outside with lashes on the rim. The eyelashes filter large particles and help to protect the eye. There is a third eyelid at the corner of the eye, this moves across the eye to spread the tears and remove dust particles. The third eyelid becomes prominent in horses with tetanus. The eyeball is made up of three layers.

The white of the eye is the tough outer sclera which becomes part of the transparent cornea at the front of the eye. The junction between cornea and sclera is the limbus. Light enters the eye via the cornea. The conjuctiva becomes transparent at the front of the eye to form part of the cornea. The middle layer, the choroid contains blood vessels, and has a central hole or pupil. Surrounding the pupil is the pigmented iris. Muscles in the iris alter the shape of the pupil to allow the correct amount of light to enter the eye. The pupil becomes narrower in bright light and dilated and rounded in poor light. The edges of the iris have irregular shaped projections, the corpora nigra, which hang over the pupil. Behind the iris is the ciliary body which contains the muscles that alter the shape of the lens. The transparent lens is attached to the ciliary body by the suspensory ligament.

The lens and ciliary body divide the eye into the anterior and posterior chambers which contain two distinct forms of fluid. The anterior chamber contains a watery aqueous humour and the posterior chamber has a thick fluid, the vitreous humour.

The retina is the thin, inner light-sensitive layer containing many nerves and blood vessels. The nerve fibres leave the eye, via the optic discs, in the optic nerve. The rods and cones, light sen-

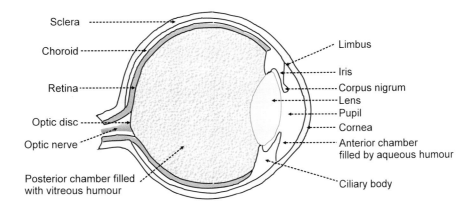

Fig.33. The internal structure of the eyeball.

sitive cells in the retina, release chemicals to cause nerve impulses that are translated into images by the brain.

Common conditions of the eye

Inflammation

Inflammation to any structures of the eye will result in swelling and pain. The eye will close when it is painful and there will be an increase in tear production (epiphora). Inflammation may be a result of an injury, a foreign body or infection.

Conjunctivitis

Inflamed conjunctiva will be swollen and red. The eye may be closed and painful with tear overflow. There are many causes including respiratory diseases when both eyes will be involved. Foreign bodies such as grass awns or dust and trauma may affect one eye. Allergies and infections are usually bilateral. Wind and flies may cause irritation and conjunctivitis.

Keratitis

Keratitis, inflammation of the cornea, may follow conjunctivitis or be a primary infection or secondary to injury of the cornea. This is extremely painful as the cornea is well supplied with sensitive nerves. There will be clouding of the cornea and the eye will be closed. Usually there is a copious occular discharge which may become purulent. Early treatment is needed to prevent permanent scarring and reduction in vision.

Uveitis

Uveitis is an inflammation of the uveal tract, (iris, ciliary body and choroid) and is serious. It is commonly caused by trauma and the cornea may also be involved.

Equine recurrent uveitis (Periodic Ophthalmia or Moon Blindness)

This is one of the most important disorders of the eye. It is found in all breeds and ages

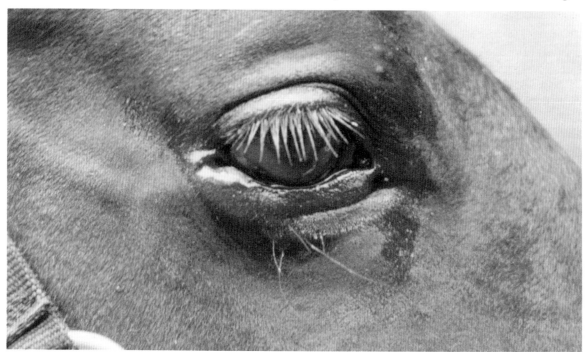

Epiphora plus an eyelid injury

of equine and occurs in all countries. The actual cause is not known but it is thought to be a response to an immune-mediated inflammation. Both eyes may be affected alternately or at the same time and the condition recurs at irregular intervals. The consequence of repeated attacks is a distorted iris due to adhesions between the iris and the lens. The eyeball becomes shrunken and covered by the third eyelid and the animal will be blind. In the acute phase the eye is extremely painful due to the corneal swelling (oedema), keratitis, uveitis and inflammatory debris in the aqueous humour.

Prompt treatment is needed to limit the damage to the eye. Unfortunately it is not possible to predict when the next attack will occur so the prognosis is guarded. Partially sighted animals require special care when handling.

Corneal injuries

Injuries to the cornea are common due to the prominence of the eye. Even though the horse has a good blink reflex it can still injure the eyes in hedges, and on sharp pieces of

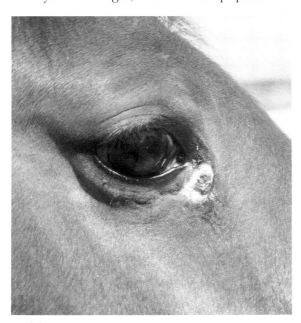

Eyelid tumour

bedding or forage. Chemical irritants like ammonia and sprays may damage the cornea. Dust and grit may be blown into the eye on a windy day. Signs of a corneal injury are:

> pain
> profuse lacrimation
> partially closed eye
> sensitivity to light
> cloudy cornea with prominent blood vessels

The eye needs to be thoroughly examined and treated according to the diagnostic findings.

Eyelid injuries

Damage to the eyelids will result in corneal problems if they are not treated promptly. They often require suturing to prevent distortion of the lids and to enable them to function correctly.

Blocked tear-ducts

The upper part of the tear-duct is enclosed in a bony canal in the maxillary bone. Swelling of the bones or inflammation of the duct will cause narrowing or blockage resulting in epiphora (tear overflow).

Occasionally horses are born with incomplete tear ducts and no opening into the nostril. Injuries to the head may also damage the tear-duct.

The patency of the duct can be tested by placing a dye into the eye and waiting for it to appear from the nasal ostium (opening in nostril).

A catheter can be placed into the nasal ostium and flushed with warm saline solution which should appear at the eye.

It may be possible to flush out debris while using this method to test if the duct is blocked.

Tumours

Masses on the eyelids and surrounding tissues are relatively common. It is important to diagnose which type of tumour is present as this will affect the treatment and prognosis. They may distort the eyelid and prevent its normal function resulting in other eye disorders. Eyelid tumours are serious as they will become larger and cause complications. The commonest tumours at this site are sarcoids, squamous cell carcinoma, melanoma and neurofibroma. They may be treated surgically, by radiation therapy, chemotherapy and immune methods depending on the tumour.

Cataracts

Cataracts are opacities in the lens. Some animals are born with cataracts, i.e. congenital cataracts, but more usually they are a result of uveitis, trauma or old age. Some are small, non-progressive and of no consequence. Mature cataracts in adult horses usually progress and eventually result in blindness. Progressive loss of sight will result in behaviour changes and clumsiness and be noticed by the owner. Diagnosis can be made by the veterinary surgeon.

Examining the eye

A horse with a painful eye will resent examination of the eye. It will usually be sedated and given analgesia (pain relief). This may be adequate in some cases but others will require an

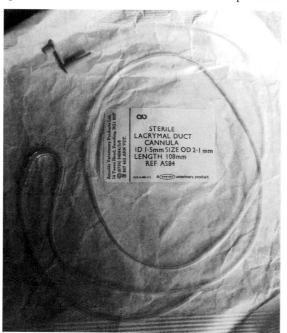

A catheter

auriculo-palpebral nerve block with local anaesthetic. This block is used to overcome the eyelid closure which prevents detailed examination of the painful eye. Local anaesthetic drops may also be instilled onto the eye surface.

The horse is usually placed in a darkened stable and all the eye structures are examined through an ophthalmoscope. Fluorescent drops are placed on the eyeball to illuminate areas of corneal damage. The dye fluoresces bright green in ulcers or blemishes. The lids and surrounding area are also inspected. Where infection is suspected, swabs from the corneal surface and from any occular discharges can be tested at the laboratory. Biopsies may be taken from tumours for histological analysis.

Treatment and medication

It may be difficult to apply medication either as drops or ointments to the eye if the patient will not co-operate. Solutions give a high level of drug release for a short period of one to two hours. Ointments give a low level of drug release for about four hours. In the acute stage it may require treatment every hour and the horse may become fractious. It is difficult to open tightly closed eyelids.

There are two types of indwelling catheters used in the horse so that there is no need to handle the eye and distress the animal. These are remote ways of delivering drugs onto the eye surface. One system is placed into the tear-duct, i.e. a nasolacrimal catheter, and the other, a sub-palpebral lavage system is attached under the upper lid. The vet will normally fit a catheter system after examining the horse and while it is sedated.

Antibiotics and anti-inflammatory solutions can be injected into the catheters. Horses with profuse epiphora will wash the drugs away or at least dilute them. The presence of pus may prevent some drugs from being absorbed.

In cases of corneal injury the eyelids may be sutured together or the third eyelid sutured across the eye to promote healing. (See nursing, page 138.)

THE MUSCULOSKELETAL SYSTEM

The musculoskeletal system includes all the structures involved in movement, i.e. the bones of the limbs and spine and the associated muscles, tendons and ligaments with their blood vessels and neurological supply. Disorders of this system result in alteration in gait and movement, i.e. lameness.

Anatomy

The horse has evolved over millions of years to walk on the tip of a single digit. The bones of the middle toe, the third digit in prehistoric horses, elongated and became the specialised structure we know today. The equine digit comprises the third metacarpus/metatarsus, the first, second and third phalanx with the proximal and distal sesamoid bones. The second and fourth metacarpal/metatarsal bones (medial and lateral splint bones) are all that remains of the second and fourth digit along with the ergots. The chestnut is the rudimentary first digit. See figure 1 page 1 and figure 23 page 34.

The foot

This consists of the hoof capsule and the structures within it. The pedal bone is suspended within the hoof by interdigitating sensitive and insensitive laminae. The pedal bone articulates with the second phalanx and the navicular bone (distal sesamoid) at the distal interphalangeal joint (coffin joint). The pedal bone is semicircular in the front feet and oval in the hind feet in horses and ponies. In the donkey all four feet are staple shaped. Ligaments bind the bones together. The deep digital flexor tendon (DDFT) attaches to the pedal bone and is separated from the navicular bone by the navicular bursa. The bursa contains synovial fluid and facilitates the movement of the DDFT over the navicular bone. The common digital extensor tendon attaches to the extensor process of the pedal bone. Cartilages are attached to the medial and lateral side of the pedal bone and can be palpated above the coronary band at the heel. The fibro elastic digital cushion lies above the frog and between the collateral cartilages.

The hoof wall, the sole, frog and bulbs of the heel are a type of modified epidermis. The horn tubules are produced at the coronary band from the dermal papillae, and with the intertubular horn, form the hoof wall. The wall is thickest at the toe and becomes thinner and more flexible over the quarters and heel. The heels expand when the foot is weight bearing. The heel wall turns inwards to form the bars of the foot. The sole, formed from the solar corium, is concave to prevent bruising and is often more vaulted in the hind feet than the front feet. The solar horn is softer and flakier than the wall due to a higher moisture content. The triangular frog is made of a more elastic, rubbery horn than the sole. It is separated from the bars by the collateral grooves and has a central sulcus.

The white line is the junction between the wall and the sole on the underside of the foot. It allows some movement between these structures and can be stretched in certain conditions which allows infection to enter the hoof capsule.

The hoof wall can be divided into three layers:

The stratum externum or the periople is composed of tubular and intertubular horn and has a high lipid content. It controls the moisture content of the hoof and protects the underlying layers.

The stratum medium is the largest layer and has zones of tubules and intertubular horn.

The stratum internum is composed of the interlocking laminae (leaves) of the epidermal (horn) and dermal (sensitive/vascular) tissues. The dermal laminae are attached to the pedal bone. Factors which affect horn quality and growth rate are discussed in part one, page 33. Incorrect foot balance and foot trimming can distort the hoof capsule, cause lameness and predispose the foot to certain diseases.

Conditions of the foot

Pedal sepsis

Infections in the foot are caused by a variety of organisms. Foot abscesses are a common cause of lameness in all equines. The animal becomes progressively lame over several hours. The foot may be hot with a strong digital pulse. Sometimes the lower limb becomes filled (swollen) and the horse will rest the foot with just the toe on the ground.

Infection may gain entry through a damaged white line or puncture wounds to the sole of the foot. If the infection is trapped between the horny sole and the sensitive tissue it causes pain as the pus accumulates and undermines the sole. The subsolar abscess can be drained and in most cases the horse will soon recover. The overlying horny sole is pared away to allow drainage and the foot tubbed in hot water and covered in a foot dressing. (See pages 131–2). A rubber or plastic boot will protect the dressing. The farrier will usually remove the shoe as it tends to cut through the foot dressings or he may alternatively reshoe the foot with a hospital plate under the

A removable hospital plate under the shoe

shoe, which allows access to the injury for inspection and replacing dressings. When the horse is sound it may be exercised on a dry surface. Animals will need tetanus antitoxin if they are not vaccinated with tetanus toxoid. Infections of the white line tend to track up the wall and burst out at the coronary band if untreated. This condition is known as gravel.

Deep penetration or puncture to the middle area of the foot is, however, very serious as vital structures, e.g. the navicular bursa, coffin joint

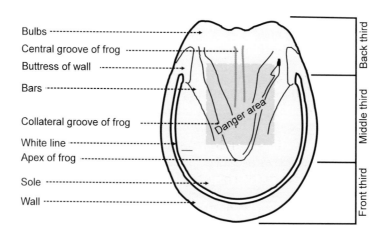

Fig.34. The ground surface of a foot to show the danger area for penetrating injuries.

Fig.35. Sagittal section of the foot.

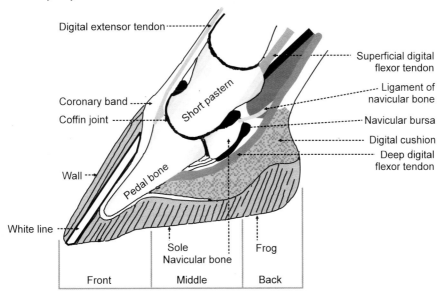

DDFT may be involved. Infections in these structures are difficult to drain and control and often result in euthanasia on humane grounds. All cases of puncture wounds need prompt attention by a vet with the correct treatment. Deep penetrations will involve surgery in order to save the patient. Cases are more likely to respond if treated early, i.e. within two days. Cases with an injury that is over seven days old have a poor prognosis.

It is important to know the anatomy of the foot so that the possible consequence of any injury is realised. If the horse is found with a nail stuck in the foot, the location, depth and angle of the nail should be noted as it is removed. This will be valuable information for the vet. In cases where the cause of penetration is unknown, deep punctures will be probed and X-rayed to locate the tract. The foot may be anaesthetised with local nerve blocks to allow more detailed exploration of the tract. Samples of synovial fluid from the digital tendon sheath and the coffin joint can be examined for signs of sepsis.

Broad spectrum antibiotics and analgesics will be needed with surgical drainage and foot dressings.

Although injuries to the foot cannot always be prevented, daily foot care will mean early detection of any potential problem.

Quittor

Injuries to the back third of the coronary band over the quarters and heel may result in quittor, which is an infection of the collateral cartilages. Pus discharges from tracts in the heel area above the coronary band. The cartilages have a poor blood supply so antibiotic therapy is not normally successful and it is difficult to get adequate drainage. Surgery is normally necessary to remove all the infected and necrotic tissue. Any injuries in the region of the cartilages that do not respond to conservative treatment should be investigated for quittor.

Thrush

Thrush is an anaerobic infection of the frog horn and the collateral grooves. The organisms destroy the horn tissue and produce a black, foul smelling discharge. In severe cases the horse will

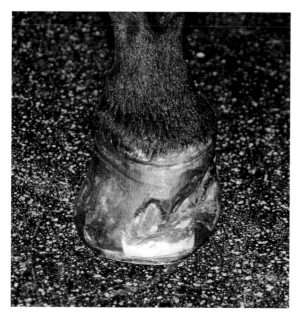

Hollow hoof disease

be lame as the sensitive tissue under the frog and sole is exposed. Commonly the hind feet are most badly affected. Thrush is a result of poor foot care, poor stable hygiene and poor management.

Both the veterinary surgeon and the farrier may be involved in the treatment. All the necrotic material is pared from the infected area which is then cleaned and dressed. It is important to keep the feet dry and replace the dressings daily. Grease, tar and oils should not be applied to the feet as they trap moisture in the hoof and prevent air reaching the tissues.

The stable floor should be power cleaned and a new, dry bed supplied. This should be mucked out every day and the unaffected feet picked out twice daily.

Onychomycosis (hollow hoof disease)

A variety of anaerobic organisms which destroy horn are responsible for this condition. The first signs are seen as grey or brown powdery areas in the stratum medium. If these areas are not removed the infection will invade the wall, creating large cavities, hence the name hollow hoof disease. It may be necessary to remove large areas of the overlying wall to gain access to the infected horn. This condition is potentially serious as the organisms are resistant to many topical antiseptics. Often animals have lesions in all their feet and will be lame. If hoof walls are resected, glue-on surgical shoes may be used once the disease is under control. Synthetic hoof fillers are not used as they may trap organisms in the foot.

A high standard of stable hygiene is required with continual foot care for many weeks. This is a time consuming and expensive condition to treat.

Poor foot care and poor stable hygiene may predispose animals to onychomycosis. Some animals have a history of seedy toe, chronic founder and white line separation, all conditions which result in poor quality horn. It is necessary to treat any concurrent disorders and provide a good diet with supplementation to promote horn growth. Animals that have genetic horn defects are susceptible to this condition and have a very poor prognosis.

Shoeing and related problems

Nail bind and nail prick are both caused by incorrectly placed horseshoe nails by the farrier. These are normally removed and repositioned immediately but occasionally they are missed and the horse is lame after shoeing. Nail bind is caused by pressure when a nail is placed too close to the sensitive laminae. A nail prick is caused by a nail puncturing the sensitive laminae and may lead to a foot abscess.

Corns

Corns occur on the sole between the wall and the bar. They are caused by abnormal pressure on the sole and are usually due to poor shoeing and long shoeing intervals. As the hoof wall grows the shoe is pulled onto the sole at the heel. Corns are normally found in the front feet, especially if the feet are shod with a shoe that is too small and too short. Feet that are not balanced and those with lowered heels are also prone to corns. Studs

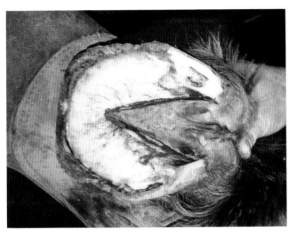

A dry corn

of sole will be discoloured and may become infected. The horse will be lame. Repeated bruising to the horny sole will eventually damage the pedal bone. This can be diagnosed radiographically.

Collapsed heels

Collapsed heels and long toes are a common fault in certain breeds that have a low heel, flat foot conformation. They can be a result of incorrect trimming and fitting shoes which are too short. The hoof pastern axis is broken back. The horn tubules at the heel will be curved under the foot and no longer parallel to those at the toe. The horse will bruise its sole and tear the laminae apart at the toe. The horse's weight will be shifted onto the heels, causing further damage and putting strain on the flexor tendons.

The foot balance has to be corrected and surgical shoeing may be required.

Cracks in the hoof wall

Cracks may be found in the hoof wall of both shod and unshod feet. Cracks that start at the

cause a mediolateral imbalance and corns may occur on the second impact side as this side takes more weight. Animals with mediolateral imbalance may eventually develop sheared heels. Stones may jam under the shoe at the heel and cause trauma at the seat of corn. Shoes with pencil heels are more likely to cause corns. On examining the seat of corn, i.e. the area of sole between the wall and the bar, three different types of corn may be seen:

1 Dry corn. Red staining of the sole due to haemorrhage of the underlying dermal tissue.
2 Moist corn. Serum accumulates beneath the damaged horn.
3 Septic corn. The horn is infected and the area becomes necrotic.

Corns are treated by removing the shoes and paring away infected and damaged horn. The horse should not be ridden until it is sound and correctly shod, i.e. wide at the quarters and heels with plenty of length. The horse should be reshod every four to five weeks or as often as the farrier advises. It is false economy to leave long shoeing intervals but a common fault with many owners.

Bruised sole

The sole may be easily bruised if the horse is flat footed or has thin soles. Animals working on rough terrain can bruise their feet on stones. This can occur in shod and unshod animals. The area

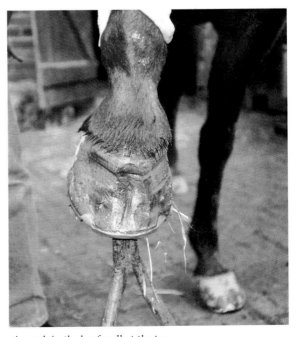

A crack in the hoof wall at the toe

ground surface are called grass cracks and those that start at the coronary band are sand cracks. Superficial cracks do not cause lameness. Deep cracks may involve the sensitive laminae, become infected and will result in lameness. The horn at the ground surface at the toe is both older and thicker than that at the heel, so the prognosis will differ depending on the position and depth of the crack.

· Cracks may be a result of an injury, especially at the coronary band, or due to irregular trimming and overlong feet. Brittle feet and thin walls are more susceptible to cracks.

Cracks caused by neglect can be prevented. Horses with brittle feet should be frequently trimmed and the feet watered and washed each day to encourage retention of moisture. Glue-on shoes are preferable to metal shoes as the nails cause further damage to the walls.

Superficial cracks can deteriorate into deeper, serious cracks and require early treatment by corrective trimming and shoeing to remove tension across the crack. Both the vet and the farrier will be required to treat deep cracks. They will remove infected horn, place filler in the defect and stabilise the hoof capsule with a surgical shoe.

Laminitis

Laminitis is a condition of the domesticated equine. It is a serious, painful disease of the foot which affects all ages and breeds of horse, pony, donkey and mule. Any number of feet may be involved and it may occur at any time of the year.

Trigger factors cause the lamellar attachments that suspend the pedal bone within the hoof wall to disintegrate. They activate metalloproteinase enzymes (MMPs) which destroy the basement membrane. This is the layer of cells which connects the epidermal cells of the inner hoof wall to the connective tissue of the pedal bone. The capillaries that supply the lamellae are also damaged and anoxia (lack of oxygen) causes more cells to die. The remaining blood supply is diverted away from the capillary network and shunted through arteriovenous anastomoses which dilate in response to the damage. The horse will have a pounding digital pulse in the affected limbs and will show varying degrees of

Founder case – a prolapsed pedal bone fitted with a heart bar shoe (R. A. Eustace)

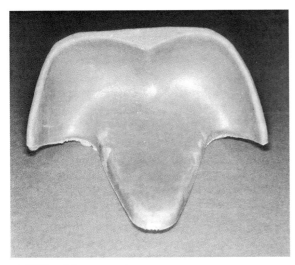

A LILY pad frog support

foot pain depending on the extent of the lamellar damage and the instability of the pedal bone.

A number of conditions appear to trigger laminitis:

1 *Nutritional*
   Carbohydrate overload due to excess cereal starch or excess soluble carbohydrate found in fast growing grass disturbs the gut flora. The normal bacteria die in the acid conditions releasing toxins which are thought to activate MMP.
2 *Trauma and mechanical damage*
   Fast work on a hard surface may precipitate laminitis. Overlong toes cause tearing of the lamellar attachments each time the foot breaks over. Animals that are lame for other reasons, e.g. fracture, may develop laminitis in the opposite foot, which is taking more weight than normal.
3 *Systemic disease*
   Retained placenta, hepatitis, respiratory infections, and diseases of other organs can all precede laminitis.
4 Cushing's disease, hyperlipaemia and steroid therapy all alter glucose metabolism and increase MMP production.
5 Travel stress and other causes of stress, e.g. colic surgery may precipitate laminitis due to release of steroids from the adrenal glands.
6 Certain drugs precipitate laminitis, especially in high risk animals, e.g. steroids.

High risk animals are those who have suffered previous attacks of laminitis, animals that are overweight, animals on free access to lush grazing and those with poor foot care/overlong feet.

The early signs of laminitis are foot pain and a pounding digital pulse. The temperature of the feet is not a reliable sign of laminitis. The coronary band may be painful and the sole is sensitive to pressure.

The animal will be lame. Mild cases will move awkwardly on uneven ground but appear normal on soft level ground. As the pain increases, the horse may shift weight from one foot to another and try to take more weight on the heels of the foot and on the unaffected feet by placing them further forward. Eventually the horse will become rooted to the spot or lie down. Animals in pain will have an elevated pulse and respiratory rate and there will be signs of the disorder which has triggered the laminitic attack.

The pedal bone may tip downwards and leave an obvious depression at the coronary band opposite the toe. This stage is called founder. The pedal bone can prolapse through the sole in front of the point of the frog, which is serious but can be treated. In severe cases the pedal bone becomes detached and the depression is felt all the way around the coronary band. These cases are sinkers and need urgent, specialised treatment within a few hours if they are to survive.

Even the mildest case of laminitis should be treated with some urgency as it can rapidly deteriorate. The horse should not be walked as movement will cause more laminar (lamellar) attachments to breakdown.

In older cases of chronic founder there is distortion of the hoof capsule and diverging growth rings on the hoof wall. The rings are closer together at the toe than the heel. There is reduced blood supply and jamming of the coronary band at the toe so the heel horn grows faster than the toe horn. The white line becomes stretched at the ground surface and is susceptible to infection. Seedy toe is a common sequela to laminitis. The sole becomes flatter and in some cases convex as the tip of the pedal bone rotates downwards.

All laminitis cases should be stabled on a deep, clean, white shavings bed with easy access to hay and water. They should be moved in a trailer to the stable and not forced to walk. They should never be starved but given the correct forage diet

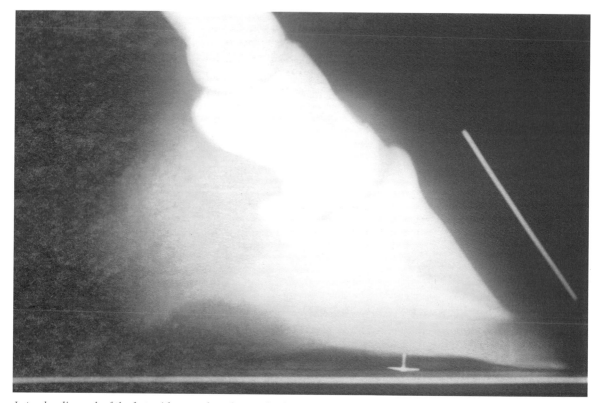

Lateral radiograph of the foot with a metal marker on the dorsal hoof wall and a pin near the point of frog (R. A. Eustace)

with supplements to promote horn growth. Overweight animals need careful dieting using a straw/hay mix. Starving obese animals can precipitate hyperlipaemia, a fatal metabolic disorder. Veterinary assistance should be sought if laminitis is suspected. The vet will provide frog supports to stabilise the pedal bone and give analgesics and medication to improve the circulation to the lamellae. Cases of toxaemia will require antibiotics. Liquid paraffin or bran mashes can be used to move the food quickly through the gut. Blood samples are taken to detect disease in other organs.

Animals with depressions at the coronary band will require foot X-rays to assess the position of the pedal bone. Glue-on adjustable heartbar shoes can then be fitted. Metal heartbar shoes may be used at a later stage when the horse can tolerate nailing on. A large amount of serum can collect under the hoof wall and this can be released by drilling a small hole in the middle of the dorsal hoof wall, which gives pain

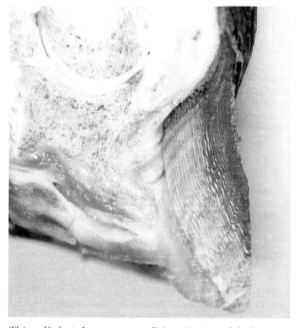

This split foot shows osteomyelitis, crimping of the horn tubules and a loss of pedal bone (R. A. Eustace)

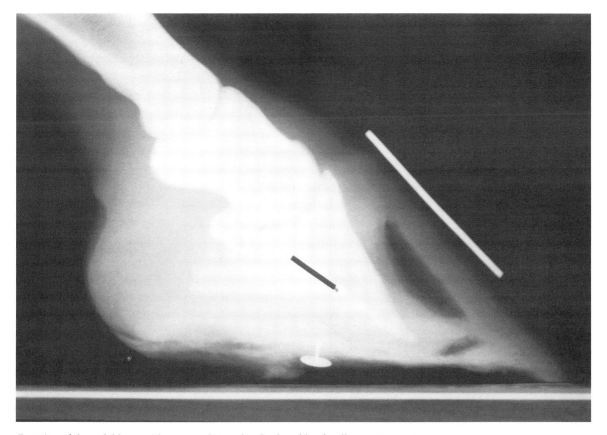

Rotation of the pedal bone with a gas pocket under the dorsal hoof wall (R. A. Eustace)

relief as it reduces pressure. It is sometimes necessary to remove the front of the hoof wall to encourage the new wall to grow parallel to the front of the pedal bone. This also improves the circulation at the coronary band and allows the serum and necrotic debris to escape. Dorsal wall resections are performed by the vet at the old founder stage, e.g. when the acute stage is over.

Animals with rotated pedal bones may have their DDFT cut so that the pedal bone is no longer under tension. These animals are fitted with heel extension shoes after the surgery.

Horses with chronic founder may become permanently lame with loss of pedal bone, osteomyelitis and deep abscess formation. These animals are crippled and are destroyed on humane grounds. All cases of laminitis need a high level of foot care and management for the

rest of their lives to avoid another attack. Careful attention to the diet and regular foot trimming are vital. Heart girth and body weight measurements taken at weekly intervals are useful to show fluctuations in weight. Mild cases will need about six weeks' box rest and gradual return to work, with restricted grazing for obese animals.

Severe founders and sinkers can take a year of dedicated veterinary, farriery and nursing care to recover.

Research in Australia on MMP inhibitor substances is underway. Recent studies have suggested monitoring the pH of faeces of grazing animals in order to anticipate carbohydrate overload. The animals are prevented from grazing when the faecal acidity increases.

A number of parameters are used to give an accurate prognosis, especially for founder cases.

The founder distance, that is the distance

the pedal bone has dropped within the hoof capsule, can be measured on X-rays with a metal marker on the dorsal hoof wall. Retrograde venography is used to detect reduced capillary perfusion by injecting dyes into the foot veins before X-rays are taken. Areas without a capillary network cannot survive.

Navicular syndrome

This is a chronic progressive disease which affects the navicular bone, navicular bursa and DDFT in one or both front feet. All breeds and types of horse and pony can be affected, especially those in seasonal or irregular work, e.g. polo, hunting.

This disease has caused confusion and disagreement in its aetiology, pathogenesis, radiographic findings and treatment, and has been used as a dumping ground for undiagnosed forelimb lameness.

The owner often observes that the horse is reluctant to work as there is pain in the back of the foot. At rest the animal may point the affected foot and weight shift. They will prefer to stand with bedding under the heel and the hind feet will be placed further under the body and base wide.

At walk and trot there is an intermittent lameness that increases on a circle. There is an alteration in stride length with the toe landing first. The strides tend to be stilted and hesistant and there may be muscle loss over the shoulder(s).

The farrier may observe an alteration in shoe wear and foot size and shape. The foot becomes more boxy with contracted heels. The horse may become unco-operative when the farrier is clenching up. Often animals with navicular disease have poor mediolateral balance, a broken hoof pastern axis and fetlock valgus or varus. Their shoes are often too short and are not supporting the back of the foot.

On examination a number of clinical tests are performed: foot percussion, hoof testers, pressure on DDFT, extension and flexion tests.

Local analgesia, nerve blocks with local anaesthetics are used to locate the seat of pain. The palmer digital nerves, the coffin joint and the navicular bursa can all be anaesthetised. Radiographs are taken to detect abnormalities in the navicular bone.

The treatment of navicular disease depends on the degree of damage found. Early cases may respond to farriery to correct foot balance and special shoes, e.g. eggbar, rolled toes, heel wedges. A regular exercise regime is important. Medication using drugs to improve the circulation and thin the blood and analgesics have all been tried. Surgery to cut the nerve supply (neurectomy) to the foot was fashionable at one time. Some cases respond to cutting the navicular suspensory ligament.

At present there is no 'cure' for this condition especially for cases that show radiographic changes to their navicular bones. Animals with a low heel and long toe conformation put more strain on the back of their foot and need careful farriery. Good shoeing, foot balance and regular exercise may prevent or slow down the progress of this condition.

Sidebone

The cartilages at the back of the pedal bone are normally springy. Sidebone is ossification of the cartilages so they feel hard and will not move. This may be an ageing process or due to concussion, foot imbalance, or an injury. This usually occurs in the front feet.

Animals are not often lame. Sometimes there is pain if pressure is applied over the developing sidebone. Occasionally they fracture; this will be painful and the horse will be lame. Lame animals should be rested, their feet balanced and the fracture treated as advised by the vet.

Bones

The skeleton has bones of various shapes and types, e.g. long, flat short and irregular. The long limb bones (appendicular skeleton) are a system of levers for converting muscular contraction into movement. The scapula and pelvic girdle contain large flat bones that provide a large surface for muscle attachment and support the axial skeleton and trunk between the four limbs. Sesamoid bones such as the patella, proximal sesamoids and navicular bone alter the pull on tendons and reduce the friction between tendons and bones. The internal organs are protected by the thoracic and pelvic girdles. Bone is an important source of calcium, phosphorus and magnesium. The red bone marrow of young foals produces red blood cells.

The long limb bones are tubular and can resist bending, tension and compression due to their biphasic structure of a mineral component to give strength, and collagen fibres to provide flexibility. Immature bone needs mechanical stimulation provided by normal forces to develop correctly. It has a higher fibrous content than mature bone, and a lower mineral content.

Bones increase in length by the production of cartilage at the growth plate which is converted to bone. The epiphyseal growth plates of each long bone ossify and close at different times. They are all closed by the time the foal reaches maturity at about three years of age. Osteoblasts that line the periosteum are responsible for the increase in diameter of the bone.

Bone consists of an outer membrane, the periosteum, which is well supplied with a network of arteries and veins and it attaches tendons and ligaments to bone. Under the periosteum is compact bone and spongy bone. The shaft of a long bone is mainly compact bone. The centre of the shaft is the medullary cavity which contains bone marrow. Both ends of the long bone have a thin layer of compact bone covering the spongy bone. (See fig. 36 on page 94.)

Bone can be subjected to developmental and nutritional disorders, trauma and infection. Serious trauma results in a fracture. Depending on the age of the animal, the bone involved and the type and site of the fracture, surgical repair or conservative treatment is possible in many cases.

Bone infection is serious and a frequent complication following accidental wounds to limbs.

This requires early, aggressive treatment and often surgery to remove infected bone.

Periostitis

Inflammation of the periosteum, periostitis, may result from a blow or infection or tearing of the ligament or tendon attachments, e.g. sprain. There will be heat, pain and swelling over the affected area involving the soft tissues. The bleeding and resultant blood clot is invaded by osteoblasts which produce new bone. The tender, inflamed area over the new bone subsides to leave a firm, painless, hard swelling.

Splints, sore shins and ringbone are all a result of periostitis.

Splints

The splint bones are attached to the cannon bone by the interosseous ligament. Tearing of this ligament in young horses results in a bony enlargement on the splint bone, which is called a splint. Animals with poor conformation, poor action and poor foot balance are more likely to develop splints. They are more common on the medial aspect of the forelimb. Excessive work on hard ground can also predispose to splint formation. Direct blows to the splint bones will also cause a splint. Large swellings at the proximal end of the splint bone may interfere with movement of the knee. Adhesions may involve the suspensory ligament and cause lameness.

During the acute stage of splint formation the animal will be lame to some degree according to the amount of damage. Diagnosis is made on clinical findings and radiographs to show the extent of the injury.

Early treatment by cold therapy and support bandages will limit the inflammation. Non steroidal anti-inflammatory drugs (NSAIDs) and box rest are advisable. Surgery is necessary in cases of fractured splint bones and those that are encroaching on the knee joint or the suspensory ligament.

The horse can gradually be brought back into

Fig. 36. The structure of a synovial joint.

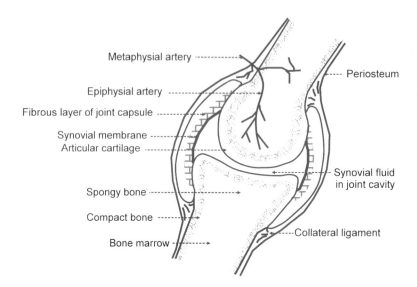

work once it is no longer lame. It should be exercised on a suitable surface and attention paid to foot balance and shoeing. Animals that move badly should wear boots to prevent brushing injuries.

Sore shins

Sore or bucked shins are seen in young horses due to the stress of work on immature bone. The area at the front of the cannon bone becomes inflamed with lifting of the periosteum, haemorrhage and microfractures. The front of the cannon becomes swollen, convex in outline and sore to touch. The horse will be lame and may take several months to recover. Treatment includes rest, cold therapy, NSAIDs to reduce inflammation and pain, and physiotherapy.

Joints

A joint is where bones meet and allows movement.

All the limb joints are synovial joints and most are capable of a large amount of movement. They are susceptible to various injuries and diseases.

The joint capsule has an outer fibrous layer attached to the outer layer of bone (the periosteum) and an inner synovial membrane which is well supplied with blood vessels and nerves. The membrane secretes synovial fluid to lubricate the joint and nourish the articular cartilage. The cartilage protects the ends of the bones forming the joint and is thickest at areas of greatest pressure.

Ligaments stabilise the joint. They can be part of the fibrous capsule and are composed of collagen and elastic fibres.

Joint sprain

The ligaments and the fibrous capsule can be torn due to twisting or turning awkwardly. In severe cases the periosteum may also be torn leading to new bone formation (callus). There will be varying amounts of heat, swelling, loss of function and pain depending on the amount of damage. There may be increased production of synovial fluid and the joint capsule will be distended. This may happen as a result of low grade trauma without causing lameness or pain, e.g. articular windgalls and bog spavin.

Articular windgalls are a distension of the fetlock joint capsule seen on either side of

A sacroiliac strain shows as an obvious bump on the croup

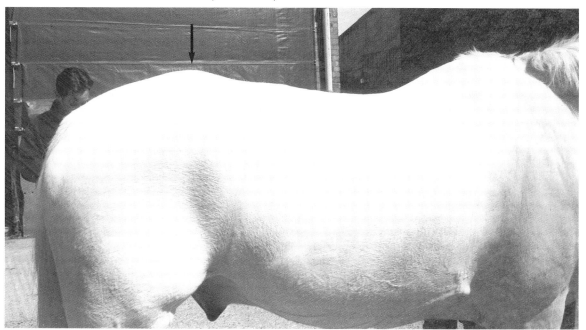

the fetlock between the cannon bone and the suspensory ligament.

Bog spavin is a distension of the tibiotarsal joint of the hock and is seen as a large swelling on the inside of the hock with a smaller swelling above the hock on the lateral side. Pressure on either swelling increases the size of the other.

They are sometimes confused with a thoroughpin. A thoroughpin is a distension of the tarsal sheath of the Achilles tendon (DDFT) above the point of the hock.

Treatment of sprains includes cold therapy, support bandages, rest, and NSAIDs. Radiographs are taken to assess periosteal damage and ultrasound scans for soft tissue damage. Physiotherapy techniques aid recovery and the prognosis is good providing the ligaments are not ruptured. Dislocation occurs when all the joint tissues are disrupted, the limb will be an abnormal shape and will be unable to bear weight.

Sacroiliac strain

The sacroiliac ligaments stabilise the sacroiliac joint between the pelvis and the sacrum. This joint is rigid in adult horses but allows a small amount of movement in young animals. It may be strained or sub-luxate due to an injury, commonly jumping. The tuber sacrale and the tuber coxae will be asymmetrical when viewed from behind. After a period of rest the injury will heal and the pelvis become stable, but horses are often left with a bump over the croup. Often animals return to work with a slight alteration in gait but are not lame.

Joint infections

Joint infections are serious and very painful with an obviously distended joint capsule. They require early treatment to avoid a septic arthritis and destruction of the articular cartilage. Bacterial infection usually follows an accidental wound but in foals may be a result of a navel infection (joint ill). Lyme's disease causes joint distension in older animals. Animals with joint infections resulting from bacteraemia will be sick, have a fever and be depressed. The diagnosis is made on clinical signs, radiography and examination of synovial fluid. The prognosis is grave unless early aggressive treatment with antibiotics and flushing the joint is effective.

Osteoarthritis or degenerative joint disease (DJD)

Osteoarthritis is a common cause of lameness especially in the distal interphalangeal joint – ringbone, and the tarsal/tarsal metatarsal joints – spavin. There are often large firm swellings around these joints due to new bone formation which are easy to see and palpate. The cause of DJD involves many factors which result in loss of a constituent, proteoglycan, from the articular cartilage. The cartilage loses its stiffness and the increased friction between the joint surfaces causes the collagen network in the cartilage to break down. Animals with conformational faults such as toe-in or toe-out or poor foot balance may contribute to the wear and tear on the joints. Certain drugs may affect the breakdown of protoeglycans and so hasten the destruction of the cartilage. Animals in irregular work or working on a poor surface are more likely to suffer joint trauma.

DJD may follow a sprain or a fracture or infection but often there is no history of such an obvious traumatic incident.

Bone spavin

This is a common cause of hindleg lameness. Usually the distal intertarsal and tarsometatarsal joints are affected. Animals with sickle hocks or cow hock conformation are predisposed to bone spavin.

Most cases have a gradual onset of lameness and present as a stiffness and reluctance to work. They are worse after hard work and after a prolonged period of rest. Usually both hocks are affected to some degree with the animal appearing to be lame on the worse leg. The horse will be shorter striding and often drag the toe which shows as abnormal wear on the shoe. It may become more difficult to shoe and resent the leg being held in a flexed position. Trotting on a hard surface will exacerbate the lameness. There may be an obvious bony swelling on the inside of the hock. Radiographs of the hock will confirm the disease. Animals in the early stages of DJD will not show radiographic signs and these cases will be confirmed by giving articular nerve blocks to abolish the lameness and analysing synovial fluid.

Treatment for spavin can vary depending on the state of the joints. Exercise, corrective shoeing, surgery and medication are all possible forms of treatment. The joints will eventually be destroyed, being replaced by bone, and will fuse together. This can take a long time but when it occurs the horse is no longer lame. Surgery aims to hasten this fusion by drilling out the joints. Some of the pain may be related to inflammation of the cunean tendon as it passes over the joint. This tendon can be cut under local or general anaesthesia. Alternatively the horse can be worked on analgesics in the hope that this will accelerate the fusion process.

Acutely inflamed joints with obvious synovial distension will require rest and further investigation.

Some horses with bone spavin will be able to do light work but will probably never return to their former athletic use.

Ringbone

This may occur in any limb but is more common in the front legs. DJD of the pastern joint is known as high articular ringbone and that of the coffin joint is known as low articular ringbone. False ringbone is new bone formation on the distal end of the first phalanx or the proximal end of the second phalanx that does not involve the joint. Horses with false ringbone may be lame initially but usually become sound once the inflammation has settled down, when they will develop a hard swelling over the affected area. Ringbone may be caused by injury to the periosteal attachment of the joint capsule and ligaments or by trauma to the periosteum. Horses with poor conformation and those in fast work involving twisting and turning are more commonly affected.

Horses with articular ringbone are lame and

Fig.37. The tendons and synovial structures of the lower limb.

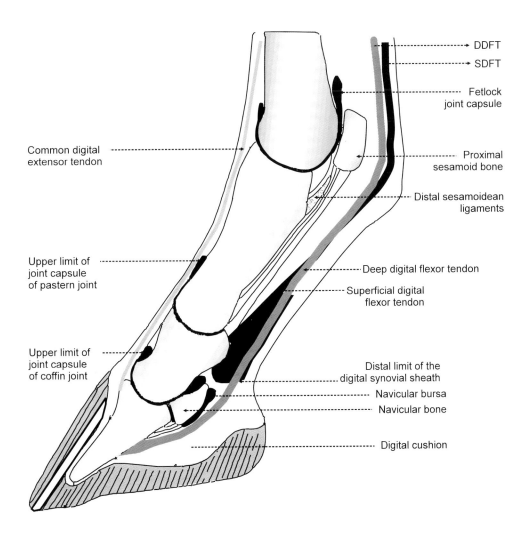

DDFT

SDFT

Fetlock
joint capsule

Proximal
sesamoid bone

Distal sesamoidean
ligaments

Common digital
extensor tendon

Deep digital flexor tendon

Superficial digital
flexor tendon

Upper limit of
joint capsule
of pastern joint

Upper limit of
joint capsule
of coffin joint

Distal limit of the
digital synovial sheath

Navicular bursa

Navicular bone

Digital cushion

will resent flexion and extension of the joint. The lameness will be exacerbated by turning sharply. There may be some heat and swelling over the pastern.

Early cases can be diagnosed on clinical examination, using nerve blocks and radiographs. Treatment by intra-articular injections of sodium hyaluronate or polysulphated glycosaminoglycan (PSGAG) in the early stages of the DJD can reduce the lameness and in the case of PSGAG, prevent further destruction of the cartilage and stimulate the repair process.

Tendons and ligaments of the lower leg

All the muscles of the horse's limbs are above the carpus (knee) and the tarsus (hock). They extend and flex the limb with virtually no rotation of the limb.

The extensor and flexor tendons attached to these muscles run parallel to the bones of the lower limb. The musculotendinous unit is responsible for limb movement and weight bearing.

There is little soft tissue protecting the lower

limb; the bones and tendons are just under the skin and are easily injured. The suspensory ligament lies behind the cannon bone; it is composed of modified muscle. It is attached to the distal row of carpal bones and the metacarpus and at the distal end to the proximal sesamoid bones (fetlock). At the fetlock it divides and passes forward to the front of the limb onto the first phalanx (pastern) where it joins the common digital extensor tendon. The suspensory ligament supports the fetlock joint.

The deep digital flexor tendon (DDFT) and the superficial flexor tendon (SDFT) are behind the ligament.

A synovial sheath surrounds the flexor tendons from above the carpal joint to the mid-

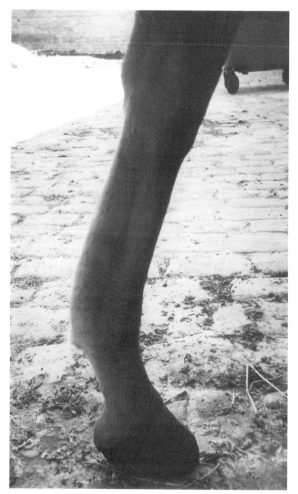

An example of a bowed tendon

metacarpal region to protect them from friction as they pass through the carpal canal at the back of the knee.

The digital synovial sheath protects and lubricates the flexor tendons as they pass over the fetlock, it extends from the distal quarter of the cannon to the middle of the second phalanx. If the digital synovial sheath becomes distended with synovial fluid the swelling can be felt above the fetlock between the suspensory ligament and the flexors. This is a tendinous windgall.

Tendons join muscle to bone. Ligaments usually join bone to bone, e.g. around joints.

The inferior check ligament (accessory ligament of DDFT) attaches the DDFT to the cannon bone. The superior check ligament attaches the SDFT to the distal radius. The check ligaments take some of the strain off the DDFT and SDFT and their muscles. They assist the suspensory ligament in supporting the fetlock joint and prevent it touching the ground when the limb is weight bearing. Any of these soft tissue structures can be overstretched, causing a strain to a tendon (tendonitis) or a sprain to a ligament (desmitis). The complete tendon or ligament may rupture or individual collagen fibres may be damaged. Haemorrhage and inflammation follows rupture of collagen fibres. White blood cells remove the damaged tissue and blood clot. Fibroblasts produce new collagen and start the repair process. This collagen is poorly aligned in the tendon and is weak. Remodelling occurs to replace the weak fibres with stronger, axially aligned collagen. This stage is assisted by controlled exercise. The collagen matures, becoming thicker and stronger. Tendons are slow to repair, taking up to fifteen months, so repeated micro injuries that occur during training can accumulate to produce quite large core lesions in apparently sound horses. These are detected by routine scanning of tendons of horses in training by ultrasound. These lesions may be due to overheating of the tendon core during fast exercise. The accumulation of micro injuries predisposes the tendon to further damage unless they are given adequate time to heal. Horses that do athletic work are prone to tendon and ligament injuries, especially the superficial flexor tendon over the mid-cannon where the tendon is at its narrowest.

Wild horses had no need to gallop for long distances as their predators were only able to sustain small bursts of speed for thirty to forty seconds. Racehorses may be required to gallop for eight or nine minutes with the extra weight of a jockey on their backs. This is expecting a lot of a structure never designed to cope with such forces. Factors that increase the mechanical overload of the tendons, will increase the incidence of injury.

Strains and sprains often occur when the horse is tired, or when the ground conditions are poor. Animals with poor conformation, poor foot balance, inappropriate shoeing and who are overweight are more likely to sustain injuries. Unfit and poorly trained horses and poor rider ability may also contribute to injury. Road work does not harden tendons but will reduce body weight.

The signs of tendonitis and desmitis will depend on the severity of the injury, e.g. mild, moderate or severe. The classic signs of inflammation, heat, swelling and pain will be apparent to some degree. These may be slight but should not be ignored: even minor strains should be treated as potentially serious. When mild injuries are not given time to heal the damage accumulates resulting in a severe injury. Animals with mild injuries may not be lame but the area will be painful on palpation and the injury will be detected using modern techniques. Ultrasound scanning, thermography, scintigraphy and magnetic resonance imaging are used to detect the site and severity of soft tissue injuries.

Animals with moderate tendon/ligament damage will be lame. Treatment is aimed at reducing the amount of swelling and inflammation and controlling pain.

Ice cold therapy with ice packs, applied over gamgee to prevent thermal burns, are used for up to three 30 minute cycles with 30 minutes of firm bandaging in between the cold treatment. The ice packs may be bandaged into place or the horse's limb placed in a cold water boot containing iced water.

Animals with severe injuries are very distressed and often cannot tolerate cold therapy. These horses should have the limb supported and immobilised to reduce swelling and prevent further injury. A Robert Jones bandage, a cast or a monkey splint may be used to keep the digits in alignment. (See page 132.)

Non steroidal anti-inflammatory drugs are used to reduce the swelling and inflammation associated with the initial injury. Other medication will reduce adhesions between the tendon and surrounding tissue such as polysulphated glycoaminoglycans. These drugs may increase the rate of healing and the quality of repair. BAPN, a scar remodelling drug is used in some cases.

Initially the horse will be on box rest with support bandages or a cast on the affected limb. Legs that are taking extra weight need checking daily. Animals with ruptured/lacerated tendons will require surgical repair and have a guarded to poor prognosis.

Therapeutic ultrasound, magnetic field therapy, laser therapy and Transcutaneous Electrical Nerve Stimulation (TENS) machines are used by physiotherapists during the repair phase. Ultrasound scanning three weeks after injury will show the extent of the injury and enable a prognosis to be given. Some cases require surgical removal of blood clots during the first week post injury and the cutting of the superior check ligament after a month.

As the tendon repairs, axial alignment of the collagen fibres is encouraged by a six to nine month graded exercise programme, initially walking in hand or on a horse walker. The time spent walking will increase by five minutes per day and build up gradually to suit the individual case over the first month. By the second month a thirty to forty minutes session in walk will be possible in most cases. The horse will be confined to a small yard or stable at all other times. After three months mild cases may start ridden exercise in walk depending on their progress. Most animals that show good progress should be back in full work in twelve to eighteen months.

Recovery is monitored by regular clinical

examination, measurement of limb diameter, gait analysis using a force plate and ultrasound scanning. Attention must be paid to the animal's diet (to prevent obesity), and to foot care.

Muscles

Muscular problems are common in the performance horse. They may be difficult to diagnose without the use of sophisticated tests to complement clinical examination and gait analysis.

Muscular injuries may be due to trauma or tearing, e.g. muscle strain, muscle rupture, muscle soreness and fibrosis. Metabolic conditions may also affect muscles, e.g. nutritional disorders, azoturia (equine rhabdomyolysis syndrome).

Diagnostic tests include blood samples to measure muscle enzyme activity and thermography to detect the site of inflammation.

Back pain

Back pain may be caused by muscle soreness or strains due to a fall or overexertion. Badly fitting saddles and poor rider ability may also result in a sore back. The skin as well as the underlying muscle may be damaged. Painful muscles will go into spasm when palpated. The horse should be rested and given NSAIDs for pain control and to reduce inflammation. Physiotherapy, heat treatment and therapeutic ultrasound will assist the recovery.

Azoturia or equine rhabdomyolysis syndrome (ERS)

This is a syndrome that affects the muscles of working horses. Exercise, diet, electrolyte imbalance and stress are thought to trigger the disease which can occur in all breeds and ages of horse. The disease tends to recur, especially if the management and diet are inappropriate. Horses with ERS show varying degrees of muscle stiffness, usually in the hindlimbs, and are distressed due to the pain. Animals may be unable to walk in severe cases hence the common name 'set fast'

which is given to this condition. Some animals will become recumbent and some will die. The horse may have hard, swollen muscles and be sweating. Urine will often be discoloured and reddish due to the presence of myoglobin, muscle pigment. Blood samples show elevated muscle enzymes in the plasma, creatine kinase (CK) and aminotransferase (AST).

It is important to prevent further muscle damage and the animal must be rested as soon as the first signs of stiffness appear. It must not be forced to walk. Often the condition appears after a short rest in the middle of an exercise session or at a competition. The horse should be transported to the nearest stable and long journeys should be avoided.

Animals with ERS may develop kidney failure so treatment involves maintaining fluid balance. Fluids may be given by mouth or intravenous drip to prevent renal failure. Urination needs to be carefully monitored and catheterisation may be necessary. The horse also needs analgesia and NSAIDs. Distressed animals require sedation so that they can be treated.

Recumbent animals need deep beds and protection from injury to prominent areas, e.g. elbows or hips. Bandages and blankets may be used for this. All cases should be kept warm and dry and fed a low energy, high fibre diet. They should have easy access to hay and water. Animals must remain stabled until they can move easily, are passing normal urine, and are free from pain on palpation of the muscles. The CK/AST levels should be monitored and the horse must not be transported long distances or put back into work until the levels are within the normal range. The horse will be allowed in a small paddock for part of each day for a week or two before ridden exercise begins. Animals that are recovering from ERS must not be given high levels of cereal grains or too much soluble carbohydrate. The energy intake must be kept lower than expected for the workload. The mineral and vitamin supplement should be analysed to make sure that a balanced diet is fed and the horse should be kept at the correct body weight. The animal must be kept warm when out at pasture with suitable rugs and shelter.

Work should start slowly with a warm-up period. Exercise on a regular basis with a slow increase in speed and intensity is important. Horses recovering from this condition will need careful monitoring in the future to avoid another bout.

Tetanus

Tetanus is a serious disease causing muscle spasm, stiffness and terminal paralysis. Tetanus is one of the earliest known diseases and over 100 years ago a Japanese scientist studied the causative organism, Clostridium tetani, in pure culture in a laboratory. The organism produces spores which can survive for years in the environment. It is found in soil, faeces and the gut of mammals. The organism cannot survive in healthy tissue; it needs anaerobic conditions to survive, so is found in damaged tissue. Wounds, however small, are a common site for the organism to multiply and release the toxin that is responsible for the muscle spasms. The toxin affects the central nervous system and the symptoms of the disease take up to fourteen days to appear.

The horse is the most susceptible of our domestic species to this life-threatening disease.

The signs of tetanus in the horse are those of a progressive stiffness and inability to eat. There is stiffness of the limbs, back and neck. The jaw muscles go into spasm hence the common name of 'lockjaw'. There is prolapse of the third eyelid and the horse will have an anxious expression with pricked ears. The nostrils will be flared and food material may be regurgitated. As the condition progresses the horse takes on a rocking horse stance, stiff legged, neck stretched out, and the tail will be raised. The horse will have a fast heart and respiratory rate and be sweating. These cases are very sensitive to noise, touch and light and the smallest stimulus will result in muscle spasm or convulsion. The horse is unable to urinate or defaecate and it rapidly loses weight due to malnutrition and dehydration. Eventually it will be unable to stand and will die of respiratory or heart failure. This disease is very difficult to treat and only animals diag-

nosed while showing the mildest signs, in the earliest stages of the condition are likely to recover. Intensive nursing in a controlled environment with sedation, antibiotics, antitoxin and fluid therapy will be required.

Prevention of tetanus is by an inexpensive vaccination course of two injections given four to six weeks apart, followed by regular boosters at one to three year intervals. The booster interval after the primary course depends on which product is used. All owners of horses, ponies, donkeys and mules should protect their animals by vaccination as they are all at risk from tetanus.

Detecting lameness

Lameness affects the posture when standing and the way a horse moves at walk and trot. It is caused by pain or discomfort somewhere in the musculoskeletal system.

Lameness may be slight, mild, moderate or severe. It may be graded from 0 to 5 where 0 is sound (not visibly lame) and 5 is severe lameness. All lame animals should receive veterinary attention. The more severe the lameness the sooner this should be provided. A lame animal is in pain, although many owners prefer to say that the horse is unlevel or stiff or 'pottery', this is avoiding the issue. Some even say the horse is stiff or unlevel but not in pain!

The vet will require details of the horse's history before examining it. These will include the age, breed or type and:

1 How long has the horse been in the owner's possession?
2 What is the exercise and management regime?
3 How long has it been lame?
4 Has it had an injury, e.g. a kick or fall?
5 When was it shod?
6 Has the lameness altered in severity?
7 Has the behaviour altered?

Lameness may be obvious when the horse is weight-bearing or when the limb is moved and the joints are flexed or extended, i.e. swinging leg lameness.

Normally 60% of the animal's body-weight is on the forelegs and the horse should stand

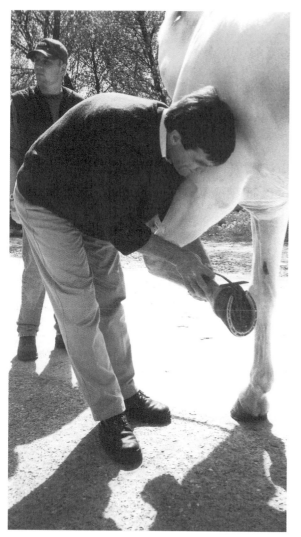

Using a T-bar to check mediolateral balance

ing the extra weight being handled. It may prefer to stand on a soft surface and may be reluctant to walk in the field or stable so all the faeces are in one spot. The horse may lie down if severely lame.

Moderate and severe lameness will be easy to detect in the standing horse and certainly at walk. If the horse is obviously lame at rest or walk there is absolutely no point in asking it to trot as this could have serious consequences.

Mild and slight lameness may be difficult to detect and probably the horse will have to be trotted in hand on both a hard and soft surface and on a gradient. The horse may be lunged on a small circle to exacerbate the lameness, turned sharply and backed to detect abnormal gait. It may be necessary to see the horse ridden to detect the problem. Some causes of lameness become progressively worse on exercise while others may wear off or become intermittent.

All the limbs including the feet should be examined for abnormal swellings, heat and pain. Digital pulses should be checked and all the joints flexed and extended to detect resistance or loss of movement. There may be signs of muscle wastage. Special attention should be paid to the wear on the shoes and the type and position of the shoes. Hoof testers may be used to squeeze each area of the sole. Defects in the hoof wall and bruising on the sole should be noted and the nails tapped with a hammer. The shoe may be removed to examine the seat of corn and the white line. In severe lameness it may be easy to locate the site of pain, especially if there is a fracture, a wound or a nail stuck in the foot. Mild and subtle lameness are harder to diagnose and need an experienced person to discover the cause of the problem. Firstly it is important to decide whether the horse is lame and then which limb or limbs are involved and finally the location of the pain.

The vet will require the horse to be handled by a competent person who is familiar with horses and confident. The horse can be held on a head-collar and rope or on a bridle with the reins over the head. The handler should wear strong shoes, gloves and a riding hat and may have to carry a short whip. Any rugs and boots should be

square with the front cannon bones vertical to the ground. The pelvis should be level and symmetrical when viewed from behind. The conformation should be assessed. When standing the horse may be resting the lame leg and only bearing weight on the toe. It may point the affected limb and not stand square. It may be taking more weight on the front or back of the foot according to the site of pain. When more than one limb is affected the horse's posture will be abnormal, the back may be arched and the hindlegs further under the body to take more weight. The horse may resent both the lame limb and the limb tak-

removed from the horse. The surface should be level, hard and non slippery.

The horse will be walked away from and turned, and then towards and past the examiner in a straight line. The handler should walk beside the horse and look straight ahead. They must not walk in front of the animal as this will obscure the observer's view. The lead rope or reins should be held loosely a metre from the horse's head so that it can move its head freely. The head movement must not be restricted in any way and the horse must not be pulled along. The horse should be turned away from the handler to change direction which enables the observer to see the horse turn and avoids it standing on the handler's toes! The foot flight pattern is noted as well as how each foot lands and leaves the ground. The length of each stride and foot height is checked. The fetlocks should all sink on weight-bearing to the same degree in the normal, sound horse.

The procedure is then repeated in trot. The trot should be active and steady. The observer must concentrate on the horse, not the handler, nor any other distractions. Dogs, small children, prams, bikes and traffic make it difficult for the examiner to focus on the horse. First listen to the footsteps. The volume and rhythm of the footfalls will not be equal in a lame animal. It is sometimes easier to listen to footfalls if you close your eyes. Less weight is taken on a lame limb so its beat will be softer, and the beat of the foot taking extra weight louder. The rhythm will be uneven, the toe of the shoe may catch the ground and this can be heard and seen. The horse is then watched as it walks and trots. The hindlimbs are observed as it goes away and the forelimbs as it comes towards you. A hindlimb lameness is seen when there is sinking or raising of the hindquarter and a shortening of the stride length. Forelimb lameness is detected by a nodding of the horse's head. In trot the nodding of the head corresponds to the sound leg taking more weight

and the hindquarters sinking. The horse is weight-bearing on the lame leg as the head is thrown up and the quarters rise. The horse may be lame on more than one limb so the action is shuffling, stilted or pottery; often the head and neck are stretched out.

Certain lamenesses are more apparent on a soft surface or on a gradient. These facilities are usually available when the lameness examination is conducted at a veterinary premises. The horse may be lunged especially if the lameness is only very slight, at trot in a straight line. Working in a small circle puts more strain on the limb on the inside of the circle and makes the lameness more easily seen. Lungeing can be done on a hard, level, non-slippery surface and on a menage. The lungeing area should be safe and properly enclosed. The horse should be fitted with a lungeing cavesson and a 7 m long lungeing rein. The person lungeing the horse should be experienced and be able to walk, trot, and stop the horse in both directions under control at all times. Some horses are evasive on the lunge and fall in on the circle, turn towards the handler, refuse to move or are difficult to stop.

Flexion tests will exacerbate lameness caused by joint pain. Each limb is held in the flexed position for one to two minutes and the handler is asked to immediately trot the horse away while the examiner looks for lame strides. Interpreting flexion tests can be difficult as more than one joint is being flexed each time. The examiner needs to take notes at all stages of the examination for comparison with any future examinations and for use after further tests, e.g. local or intra articular nerve blocks.

Diagnostic ultrasound, radiography, bone scans, arthroscopy and thermography are all veterinary techniques used in the diagnosis of lameness. Samples of blood and synovial fluid may be examined if an infection is suspected.

Video recordings and force plate analysis may also be useful in obscure cases.

CONDITIONS OF THE ELDERLY EQUINE

The life expectancy of equines varies with each species; donkeys can reach fifty years of age, ponies thirty to forty years and horses twenty to thirty years. The working life expectancy is usually much less. Insurance and feed companies refer to animals over sixteen years as being old. The general state of health and fitness of the older horse will depend on the standard of management and the type and amount of work done in its younger years. Any previous illness may lead to problems in old age. Many competition animals may not be able to pursue their particular discipline as they become elderly but may be schoolmasters or compete at a lower level which is not as physically taxing.

All horses and especially elderly animals benefit from an annual veterinary examination. This should include:

1 Blood samples for a full metabolic profile. The amount of liver and kidney enzymes in the blood are tested to detect any disease in these organs.

   The blood cells are counted to check for anaemia and chronic infections. It is very useful to have regular samples from older horses while they are in good health so that these results can be used as a bench mark to compare with any results obtained when the animal is unwell.

2 The heart and lungs should be auscultated to monitor for deterioration in any existing conditions and to detect any new problems.

3 The eyes should be examined for cataracts. Partially sighted animals should be approached carefully. The eyelids are palpated for growths. The lacrimal ducts may become blocked causing tear overflow and staining down the face. Tear staining is also a sign of vitamin A deficiency. Discharges will attract flies.

4 The teeth must be carefully examined using a gag and a torch to visualise all arcades. Sharp points, hooks and peridontal disease can be detected and treated accordingly. Some elderly equines have wave mouths and abnormalities of the incisors. Loose teeth and root fragments are extracted and tall teeth rasped to prevent them touching the opposing gum. Horses who lack good occlusion of their cheek teeth need special feed, e.g. soaked grass nuts. If the horse is unable to grind its food adequately it is predisposed to impactions of the gut which present as colic. Some horses require dental attention every three months. Most elderly equines suffer from some form of dental disease. Tumours are more common in the older horse. Prior to sedation and surgery a full clinical examination is advisable.

5 The animal should be examined for lameness. Many elderly animals have stiffness and pain in their limbs and neck. Neck pain will affect grazing, self grooming and ability to reach water and feed buckets. It may be difficult to reach and pull hay out of a net. The animal with joint pain becomes more difficult to trim and shoe. The

Dilated nostrils seen in COPD, a respiratory disease

104

pattern of wear on the shoes may alter due to an alteration in gait and limb flight patterns. The hoof horn quality may also become poorer with age, and supplementation of the diet with extra additives may be necessary. Arthritic animals need pain control to improve their quality of life. They may have weaker bone due to low phosphorus levels and are more likely to suffer spontaneous fractures and hip dislocation.

6 The skin is a common site for tumours and older equines may develop a variety of tumours, e.g. lipoma and melanoma. Elderly equines may have excessively long coats and fail to shed their coat in spring. The skin of the elderly tends to be more fragile, prone to infections and trauma, e.g. pressure sores.

7 The animal's body-weight should be regularly monitored. Animals that are inactive may become obese. Overweight animals are putting more strain on their heart and musculoskeletal system. Elderly animals may be in poor body condition due to poor dentition, pain, organ failure, anaemia and low grade infections. Weight loss may be due to gastrointestinal dysfunction. Horses over twenty years may have reduced digestion of protein, phosphorus and fibre compared to younger animals on the same ration. This may be due to previous parasitic damage which has caused scarring of the gut mucosa. There may be altered gut motility as well as reduced absorption of nutrients. Animals on medication may have reduced bacterial digestion and fermentation. Older horses may have lower levels of vitamin C, E and B complex. Prior to altering the diet of the older horse it is important to check their liver and kidney function by blood tests. Animals with hepatic and renal dysfunction will need special diets to prevent further damage to these organs. Those with chronic liver disease require a high carbohydrate, low protein diet, B complex vitamins and glucose. Animals with chronic kidney disease need a higher fat and carbohydrate intake and limited protein.

Soaked sugar beet pulp and increasing dietary fat may improve body condition. There are a number of special formulated compound feeds available for the older horse.

There are several age related conditions seen in equines. Colic caused by colon and caecal impactions are more common in horses over ten years of age. Strangulated gut caused by a fat tumour (lipoma) twisting around the intestine is the commonest surgical colic in the old horse.

Cushing's disease is caused by a tumour of the pituitary gland which is seen in the older horse.

These animals fail to shed their coats, which may be long and curly and they frequently have laminitis. They drink and urinate excessively and often have chronic infections. The diagnosis can be confirmed by blood tests and treated with pergolide or cyproheptadine and good nursing care.

Many geriatric horses have a good quality of life providing that they have the correct management.

It is important to design an exercise regime to suit each animal's capabilities in order to improve suppleness and reduce muscle wastage. Regular exercise is important, avoid fast work on hard surfaces, which jars the joints. Schooling on a prepared surface using large circles can be

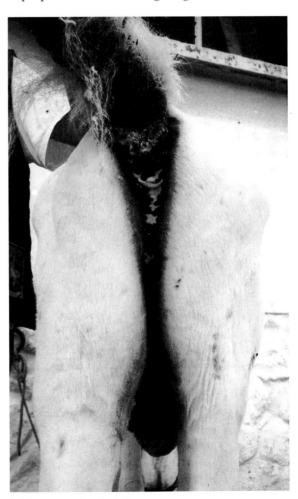

Melanoma under the tail

Pituitary adenoma causes a long, shaggy, curly coat

helpful in keeping the soft tissues supple. If the horse has a tendency to stumble, knee boots should be used for road work. Some animals who can no longer be ridden can be exercised in hand. Pain should be controlled/abolished with analgesic drugs, acupuncture, physiotherapy, massage and warmth. Solaria are very beneficial for older equines, to warm them up prior to exercise and to dry them off after exercise. Non-slip flooring and rubber mats in stables can improve the quality of life as the animal is more confident to lie down. Thick banks and large stables help prevent the animal becoming cast, as do anti-cast rollers. Travelling boots which protect the hocks and lower limbs will prevent pressure sores and rubs on animals that spend a lot of time lying down or have difficulty in getting up. Flat paddocks should be provided for lame animals.

Old horses tend to grow thicker coats and those with pituitary tumours (Cushing's disease) do not cast their coats. They require clipping to

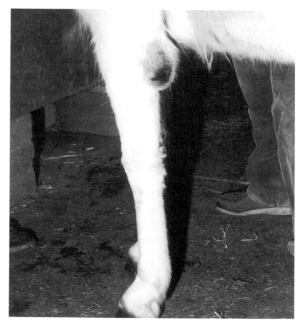

Capped elbow or hygroma

keep the hair clean and the skin healthy. They are more susceptible to skin infections and heavy lice infestation. Grooming is a form of massage and a time to look for bed sores and developing skin growths. The dock, sheath and udder should be kept clean.

Horses should not be allowed to become obese or emaciated. They should be condition scored and their body-weight assessed frequently, e.g. every two weeks. Internal parasites must be controlled, older horses need worming for encysted small strongyles in the autumn and spring and they require regular booster vaccines. They should be fed separately and may require special diets and supplements.

Many older animals appreciate being separated from young, boisterous animals to prevent bullying. They need some peace and quiet and a time to rest. They also require protection from extremes in the climate, e.g. heat stress, cold and wet conditions. They do not tolerate cold as well as younger adults. They need field shelters in summer and winter. Most older horses will be rugged in winter and even native ponies may need to be rugged up as they become older. Stabled animals can have legs bandaged for warmth and to prevent filling of the lower limbs.

Elderly equines need as much, and sometimes more, care and attention than younger animals. They certainly cannot be retired into a field and forgotten about when they are no longer ridden. Most owners will at some time have to face the time when their animal should be put down. This may be because it has a poor quality of life or a terminal illness, or to prevent further suffering due to a serious injury or disease. The veterinary surgeon can advise the owner if the time has come for humane destruction, but the final decision lies with the owner. The horse's welfare should come first so it is wise for all owners to have thought about the subject before it is forced upon them. (See page 143.)

WOUNDS

Accidental wounds are common and frequently require veterinary attention.

Wounds are usually classified as one of the following types:

1 Bruise or contusion
2 Abrasion or graze
3 Incised wound
4 Lacerated wound
5 Puncture wound

1. Bruise

A bruise is caused by a blow from a blunt object. The skin surface remains intact but there is bleeding into the skin which causes discolouration. There will be pain and swelling and there may be a blood clot (haematoma) under the skin depending on the force of the blow.

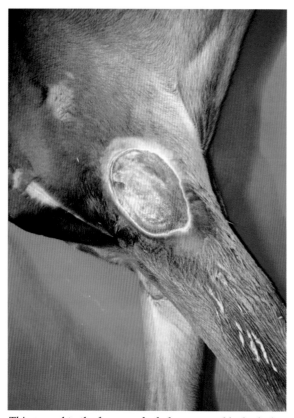

This wound to the forearm of a foal was caused by barbed wire (two weeks ago)

2. Abrasion

Abrasions are caused by friction with a rough surface. They are painful, as a number of superficial nerves are exposed. The surface of the skin is damaged with hair loss and pinpoint haemorrhage. Foreign material such as grit may contaminate the wound.

3. Incised wound

These are usually caused by a sharp flint, metal object, tin or glass. They have full thickness, clear, straight skin edges similar to a surgical incision. They may bleed profusely, especially if a major blood vessel is cut. They are not initially very painful as there is little bruising and inflammation. They may be suitable for primary closure by skin sutures if they are not grossly contaminated. Contaminated wounds must be properly cleaned and may be sutured at a later date (secondary closure).

4. Lacerated wound

These are often caused by barbed wire injuries, impaling on stakes and accidents involving traffic. Lacerated wounds have jagged skin edges, skin flaps and skin deficit. The underlying tissues, blood-vessels and nerves may be damaged and exposed. Fluid and debris collect in pockets. They often bleed profusely and are grossly contaminated. There is often skin loss and tissue death due to a loss of blood supply. These wounds require veterinary attention.

5. Puncture

Puncture wounds often initially appear to be trivial but can be very serious. The small entry hole gives no clue to the depth or direction of the tract beyond it. There can be tissue damage and debris in the tract which travels deep into the underlying tissues. This is the ideal condition for tetanus bacteria to multiply, with possible fatal consequences in the unvaccinated animal.

Puncture wounds are often complicated

A small wound to the pastern

wounds. They may involve synovial structures such as tendon sheaths, joints, or bursa. Body cavities, bones and tendons may be punctured from a small surface wound, these wounds require urgent veterinary attention.

Wounds may appear to be clean or contaminated with hair, soil, faeces etc. All contaminated wounds and even clean wounds will be infected if they do not receive attention within six to eight hours. Infected wounds will be hot, swollen and painful and there may be pus present. Complicated wounds, wounds to the eye or where there is arterial bleeding need prompt veterinary attention.

Wound healing follows certain stages:

1. The inflammatory stage
   This stage lasts from the time of injury to twenty-four hours post insult. The small blood-vessels around and in the wound constrict to limit the bleeding. Within ten minutes small venules dilate and leak blood and serum into the wound. Clots and serum plug the wound. Various types of white blood cells mop up the debris and bacteria. The skin cells at the perimeter of the wound start to multiply at eight to twelve hours. The next stage of

repair cannot commence until this stage is completed. A moist environment and a good blood supply is necessary.

2. The repair stage
   This stage takes up to seven days. In most areas where the skin is relatively loose the wound edges start to contract so making the skin defect smaller. In lower limb wounds wound contraction is very slow and starts at day fifteen post injury. The fibrin clot is invaded by fibroblasts which produce collagen fibres and a protein ground substance. The granulation tissue is highly vascular and prone to injury. It continues to be produced until it is covered by the new epithelium.

3. The maturation stage
   This is the final stage of healing. There is a reduction in fibroblasts, capillaries and collagen fibrils. The granulation tissue becomes paler and firmer. As the scar matures it becomes smaller, although it increases in strength over a long time it will never be as strong as the surrounding tissue.

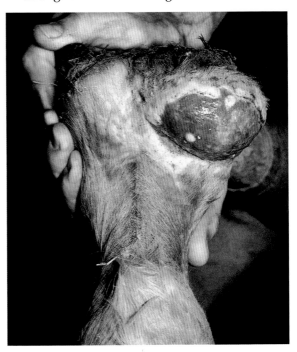

Proud flesh on the bulb of the heel (C. L. Hocking)

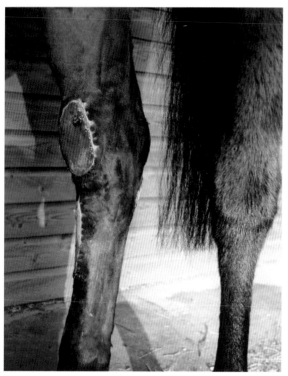

A hock wound which has granulated and is ready to receive skin grafts (C. L. Hocking)

Factors which affect wound healing are:

* The patient's age and physical status
  Elderly and debilitated animals and those with major organ dysfunction heal slowly.

* Nutrition
  The animal's diet is important, especially the protein, vitamin and mineral levels particularly in cases with a large, lacerated wound.

* Therapeutic medicines
  Local anaesthetics and anti-inflammatory drugs delay wound healing. Ointments and wound powders also delay healing.

* Trauma
  Chemicals like antiseptics and physical trauma from bedding materials, insects, or high water pressure from hoses will all delay healing.

* Infection
  Infection at any stage of wound healing will stop the process.

* Movement
  Movement of the wound edges disrupts the epithelial cells that are migrating across the defect.

* Environmental factors
  Wounds require an optimum temperature, pH, blood supply and hydration for cell activity.

First aid for wounds, see page 126.

PART THREE

EQUINE NURSING

REGISTERING WITH A VETERINARY PRACTICE

Every horse should be registered at a veterinary practice for routine health care, e.g. vaccinations, dental maintenance, worming programmes and an annual clinical examination. The practice will also supply and advise on first aid kit and insect control. Animals on the recommended health scheme are less likely to develop serious problems.

The vet will have previous knowledge of the animal, its management, the owner and the location should he be needed in an emergency. This is the advantage in registering with a practice rather than waiting until there is an emergency before making contact with a practice.

The practice will keep a record of all visits, treatment and medication given to the horse. Many practices organise equine clinical evenings on a variety of veterinary topics for their clients' benefit.

Routine visits are booked in advance and during normal office hours. Most practices have set times for arranging such visits. Emergencies may happen at any time and obviously have priority over non-urgent cases. Out of hours visits are reserved for urgent and emergency calls and there may be different phone numbers for day and night calls.

Some practices have their own surgical and hospital facilities whereas others refer cases to colleagues who are specialists in that particular field. When registering with a practice it is advisable to ask about the facilities and the arrangements for surgical or specialised procedures.

Veterinary visit

There are no set rules about when to seek veterinary advice but the owner should be aware of the significance of any signs of ill health. The first sign that something is wrong with the horse may be a change in the animal's normal behaviour and this may be quite subtle. Other signs are an alteration in appetite and thirst and therefore the quantity of faeces and urine. There may be coughing, a nasal and occular discharge and other signs of a respiratory disease. Skin diseases are usually easy to detect when grooming the horse. Digestive problems may present as colic or changes in appetite and faecal content. Lameness will be apparent on ridden exercise or when observing the horse in the field. Once a problem has been noticed, a more detailed examination is required to assess if the condition warrants immediate veterinary attention or can be easily treated by the owner. Veterinary advice can always be sought if there is any doubt and this is preferable to asking the unqualified local horse expert!

Conditions can be categorised into the following groups according to their severity:

1. Emergencies requiring immediate veterinary assistance:

   These are cases where the horse is seriously injured or is suffering from a life-threatening disease. The welfare of the animal is of paramount importance and on humane grounds all animals should receive early treatment to avoid unnecessary suffering.

   a) Serious injuries are those involving body cavities such as penetrating wounds to the chest or abdomen;
   injuries to the eye;
   wounds involving synovial structures such as joints and tendon sheaths;

puncture wounds containing a foreign body such as a nail or piece of wood;

fractures to limbs where the animal is not weight-bearing;

continuous bleeding from an injury or body orifice;

injuries to the head, neck and chest causing respiratory distress;

serious burns by fire or chemicals;

smoke inhalation.

b) life-threatening conditions include:

colic where there is an increase in pain and circulatory collapse;

acute laminitis with depressions at the coronary band;

tendon injuries;

difficult foaling;

a collapsed, staggering or unconscious animal;

suspected poisoning;

difficulty in passing urine or faeces or passing blood-tinged urine or diarrhoea;

acute respiratory distress, e.g. allergic response (SPAOAD);

high fever (39°C); heat stroke (40°C);

distress, dehydration or exhaustion after exercise.

In an emergency the vet should be given accurate information about the patient, details of the horse's location and a contact phone number.

The horse should be kept quiet and comfortable and given whatever first aid the vet has advised. While watching the horse, its vital signs can be monitored at regular intervals. It may be necessary to arrange transport for the horse as soon as the vet has examined it. Insurance companies may also need to be notified of the problem.

2. Cases that need veterinary attention the same day.

Wounds that require suturing, or are not responding to first aid or look infected, e.g. swollen and painful. Animals requiring tetanus antiserum.

Animals that are suddenly lame or obviously lame at walk or lame in more than one limb.

Loss of appetite with depression and other signs of illness.

Animals with a fever or hypothermia and other signs of illness.

Increased respiratory rate, coughing and nasal discharge.

Diarrhoea with or without colic.

Eye problems, e.g. partially closed eye, tear over-

flow, cloudy or damaged eye surface, conjunctivitis.

Intense pruritis with self mutilation and distress.

Foaling complications, e.g. retained placenta, weak or sick foal.

Dangerous or bizarre behaviour.

A clean stable with adequate lighting and hot water should be made available for the vet. The horse may need a stable rug and leg bandages and possibly a bridle to be correctly restrained for the examination.

3. Trivial or minor problems should be carefully monitored over the next twenty-four to forty-eight hours and if there is any deterioration or development of other symptoms a veterinary visit should be arranged.

Slight lameness.

Loss of appetite but otherwise bright.

Cough or soft faeces without other symptoms of illness.

Gradual loss of weight.

Non-itchy and non-painful skin lesion.

Preparation

Whenever the veterinary surgeon examines an animal for a routine procedure such as a vaccination he expects the horse to be handled by a competent adult. Children should not handle horses for veterinary procedures as even placid animals can react in an uncharacteristic manner. The horse should be presented in a clean condition and already in a stable with the handler when the vet arrives on the premises. The vet does not want to waste time searching for the animal and a handler, nor waiting for it to be caught in the field. This will make him late for the next appointment. When a routine visit is booked the appointment time will be arranged to fit in with other visits so the vet needs to know in advance how many animals he is examining at each premises. He does not want to be presented with extra animals unless they are genuine emergencies.

In the case of emergencies the animal may have to be examined in a field or on a road if it cannot be moved without veterinary supervision.

Restraint by grasping the skin at the base of the neck

Transport and stabling should be arranged while waiting for the vet to arrive.

Case history and record keeping

A detailed history of the animal is usually required. The age, sex, breed or type of animal and its description including colour, brands or freeze marks are usually kept on the practice records. The length of time it has been owned, what activity it is used for and the type of management will also be recorded. Existing ailments relating to the present problem may also be significant. It is important to know if the animal is on any medication or has a history of allergic or adverse reaction to any products. The onset, duration and progression of the present problem may help in making a clinical diagnosis. The horse may be referred to another clinician or need subsequent examinations so it is essential to have accurate written details of each examination. These details are needed for insurance claims and for calculating the account.

Methods of restraint

The owner or nurse will normally handle the horse for the veterinary examination. The animal may be in unfamiliar surroundings, be distressed, or be in pain and may be unpredictable. It has to be restrained calmly and firmly to prevent injury to itself, the handler and the vet. The handler should wear stout boots, gloves and probably a hard hat. The degree and type of restraint depends on a number of factors: the age and temperament of the patient, the level of training and the treatment/procedure for the injury or disease. The animal should be observed from a distance to assess whether it is calm or nervous, relaxed or agitated. The vet can then decide if physical restraint will be adequate or if chemical restraint should be used. It may require more than one assistant to help the vet and restrain the horse.

The horse should be in a confined area, a stable or small yard. It should be placed beside a wall to prevent it moving sideways. The handler must stand at the same side of the animal as the vet otherwise they may push the horse on top of each other. The horse may be distracted by offering a small feed or by talking quietly to it.

Buildings with a low roof or ceiling should not be used as the horse may bang its head if it panics.

The horse may be held on a headcollar and rope. The rope can be threaded over the nose-band

113

Restraint using a nose twitch

to apply pressure on the horse's nose if it becomes unruly. If the horse starts to push into the handler they can push the horse away with their elbow while still controlling the head. Some animals are badly trained and pushy but not dangerous and just need firm handling. It is not easy to control the adult horse without controlling its head and a bridle allows more control than a headcollar. A skin pinch or a nose twitch will subdue some horses. Gripping a handful of loose skin on the side of the neck just above the shoulder is a useful method of restraint for a short procedure, especially in horses that are head shy.

THE TWITCH

The top lip can be held by hand or by a humane twitch. This method is used to restrain horses for

short periods of time when sedation is not advisable. Applying pressure to the horse's lip causes the brain to release natural endorphins which relax the animal. This takes a few minutes to have the desired effect and some animals will become drowsy so the handler must pay attention. It is not advisable to twitch animals that have been sedated with drugs. Not all horses accept a twitch and some may suddenly become violent after the twitch is applied so care must be taken to avoid injury.

There are two main designs of twitch; a short wooden pole with a loop of soft rope attached to one end, and a metal humane twitch which clamps onto the upper lip and can be clipped to the headcollar. The wooden loop twitch may cut into the horse's nose if it struggles and the wooden handle can swing round which may injure the handler. To apply the twitch the loop is threaded over the hand onto the wrist and the handle held in the other hand. Standing at the side of the horse the top lip is grasped and the loop slipped over the lip. The wooden handle is twisted until the rope is held firm and won't slip off the nose. The twitch can be loosened or tightened as required and the handle must be held securely at all times. The twitch should not be left on for more than twenty minutes. Care should be taken when removing the twitch as the horse may swing its head. The horse's nose should be rubbed and checked for rope marks.

The metal twitch consists of two rounded pieces of metal which hinge together; it is easier to apply. The nose is grasped as before and the twitch is clamped onto the lip. Once in place it can be attached to the headcollar to leave one hand free. Sometimes this type of twitch can cut the nose if the skin is trapped in the hinge as the horse struggles.

THE CHIFNEY BIT

A chifney or anti-rear bit can be used on very strong animals but care must be taken to avoid damaging the animal's mouth. This is a circular bit; the top half goes into the mouth and the bottom half under the chin. A lead rope can be attached to the ring on the bottom of the bit. It should only be used by experienced handlers.

HOLDING UP A FORELEG

This method is used to keep the horse still and to prevent them kicking, especially when treating a limb. It is used in horses that are well handled. As horses are capable of standing on a diagonal pair of legs, when treating a hindleg hold up the foreleg on the same side. If a foreleg is being treated hold up the opposite foreleg. One person should hold the horse and a second person hold the leg. The horse should be stood square and the handler positioned at the shoulder facing the tail. The hand nearest the horse is run down the shoulder and the back of the foreleg to lift the foot off the ground. Horses that are reluctant to

pick up the foot will do so if the chestnut is squeezed. The leg is then held firmly with one hand below the knee and the other on the pastern. The horse must not be allowed to lean on the assistant who is holding the leg. If the horse struggles and the leg has to be released it is vital that everyone is warned to prevent an accident.

Restraining foals

Foals are not always halter broken and cannot be restrained by controlling their heads. They can injure themselves if they panic and tend to rear and rush backwards. The mare should be caught and held quietly with the foal nearby. The foal is then held with one arm around the rump and the other around the brisket and shoulder. They can be carried in this way, size permitting. They respond to having their withers scratched.

Sedation

Chemical restraint or sedation is a very effective method of calming a horse. It is used on fractious animals and for difficult procedures that require the horse to keep still. Sedation is more effective if used before the animal becomes agitated. The animal is clinically examined by the vet; the heart and lungs are auscultated. The type and dose rate of sedative is carefully chosen and usually injected into the jugular vein. The horse is placed in quiet surroundings and allowed a few minutes to become relaxed. Some sedatives cause drowsiness and make the horse unsteady on its feet so care must be taken when moving the animal. The dose rate usually affects the depth of sedation and the length of action of the drug. Sedatives may be given with analgesics.

The horse handler has a responsible job and the vet and other assistants are putting their trust in that person. It is important that they observe the horse's behaviour at all times and do not allow themselves to be distracted.

BASIC NURSING SKILLS

The horse owner is often expected to take on the role of nurse if their horse is sick or injured. Some people do not have the experience, time or facilities; in which case the horse is hospitalised at a veterinary premises.

Basic nursing involves all aspects of horse care including stable management, grooming, feeding, fitting rugs and bandages. The nurse must be able to approach and catch the horse in the stable, fit a headcollar and bridle, tie up correctly and pick out feet. The condition of the patient has to be monitored and this is normally recorded on a day chart. The nurse may be responsible for administering any medication, following veterinary instructions, observing and changing dressings and preparing equipment.

Monitoring the patient

Animals recovering from surgery should be continually observed. Intensive care is needed for colic cases, sick foals and recumbent patients. This will involve a number of people so careful record keeping is vital in order for all the treatments to be given at the correct time and any change in the animal's condition noticed and dealt with immediately. Cases that do not require intensive care may need observation every two or three hours. All observations should be recorded on the day chart. The patient's appetite, food and water intake should be recorded. The amount of urine and faeces passed and the frequency noted. The animal's behaviour, how often it moves, lies down, rolls or shows pain is significant.

The nurse will probably monitor the temperature, pulse and respiratory rate two or three times daily. Other common tests are monitoring digital pulses, capillary refill test, skin pinch test, colour of mucous membranes and monitoring gut sounds. The equipment needed for these tests includes a watch with a second hand, a clinical thermometer, jar of Vaseline, cotton wool or paper towel and a stethoscope.

It is useful to record each animal's normal vital signs when healthy for reference when they are ill. The owner should practise these tests so they are able to monitor their horse's health. The vital signs should be checked when the horse is standing quietly in the stable.

1. *Temperature*
   Do not take the horse's temperature immediately after it has defaecated. The horse can be tied up or held by an assistant. The thermometer is removed from its case and shaken so that the mercury level is lower than the graduated temperature scale. Lubricate the bulb with Vaseline. Stand close to the side of the hindquarters, run your hand over the rump and lift up the tail. Slide the bulb of the thermometer through the anus into the rectum so that it lies against the rectal wall. The

Temperature check

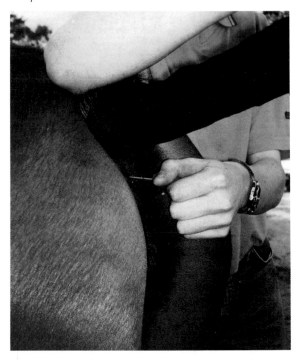

thermometer should not be placed into a fae-cal ball nor prod the rectal wall. The ther-mometer is removed after one minute and wiped clean. The temperature is read off the scale. Clean the thermometer in a cold disin-fectant solution, dry, shake down the mercury and return to its case. It should be kept in the first aid kit or a cool cupboard.

The average normal temperature for the adult horse is 37° to 38°C (98.5° to 100.5°F). Foals' and ponies' temperatures are normally higher than this, and donkeys' are at the lower end of the range.

When taking a temperature notice if the tail is flaccid and if the anus is slack.

2. Pulse rate

The pulse rate is taken when the horse is calm and at rest. The rate increases with exercise,

Checking the pulse rate

excitement, stress, pain and fever. The pulse reflects the heart rate. Any superficial artery can be used; the facial artery as it passes under the lower jaw, the median artery on the inside of the upper forelimb, the coccygeal artery on the underside of the dock, the digi-tal artery on either side of the fetlock joint. The facial artery is commonly used. The horse is held on a headcollar and should not be eating. The artery is located with the finger tips on the lower edge of the mandible, the finger pressure is adjusted until the pulse is easily detected. The number of beats are counted in 15 seconds timed on the watch. This value is multiplied by four to give the pulse rate per minute. The beats can of course be counted for a whole minute if the horse remains perfectly still. Alternatively if a stethoscope is available the heart rate can be counted. The diaphragm end of the stetho-scope is placed on the left chest wall behind the point of the elbow with the left foreleg slightly forward.

Normal resting heart-rates vary according to the age, breed, size and fitness of the ani-mal. Normal range is 25 to 45 beats per minute. Large, fit horses will be at the lower end of the range with young and smaller ponies and donkeys at the top end.

3. Respiratory rate

The quality, depth and rate of respiration can vary widely among horses. Breathing should be barely noticeable at rest in the healthy ani-mal. The breaths will be even and regular with only slight movement of the chest wall and flanks. Small movements of the nostrils may be detected.

Breathing can be observed from a distance and there is no need to handle the horse. On cold days you can see the exhaled air coming out of the nostrils.

The number of breaths in or out are counted over 15 seconds and multiplied by four to obtain the respiratory rate per minute. If both inspiration and expiration are counted you will have doubled the actual rate. The normal range at rest is 8 to 15 per minute.

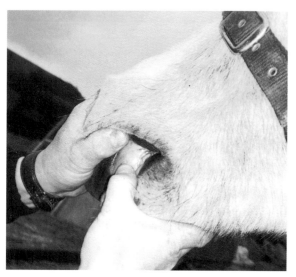

Capillary refill test

4. Digital pulses

The paired digital arteries run down the back of the leg on the lateral and medial side between the suspensory ligament and the DDFT. They can be felt as they pass over the fetlock joint. Digital pulses in all four limbs should be checked as part of the daily grooming routine before picking out the feet, particularly in animals with a history of laminitis. An increase in rate and volume of the digital pulse is an indication of inflammation or laminitis.

5. Capillary refill test and colour of mucous membranes

This is one of the tests used to indicate the state of hydration and the circulatory system.

This test is performed on the gum above the upper incisor teeth. The top lip is lifted and the colour of the gums noted. Normally the gums are pink and slippery to the touch. The gum is then blanched using the thumb and the time taken for the colour to return after releasing the pressure is counted. The capillary refill time should be less than two seconds. An increase in this time indicates a reduction in blood volume or blood pressure due to dehydration, blood loss or shock. Dry mucous membranes can indicate dehydration. The membranes may be an abnormal colour; pale, brick red, jaundiced, blue or purple which warrants further investigation.

6. Skin pinch test

This is a test to check hydration. When the horse is dehydrated water is lost from the skin which becomes less elastic. A fold of skin, usually at the point of the shoulder or the upper eyelid is gently lifted away from the underlying tissue between finger and thumb. It is twisted slightly and released without causing pain, the tent of skin should fall back into place within 1½ seconds. A delay indicates dehydration.

7. Gut sounds

Gut sounds are evaluated by listening over the upper and lower flank on both sides of the abdomen. These sounds vary in frequency, quality and character in the normal horse depending on when it last ate or exercised. Practice is needed to know the normal range of sounds. Absence of sounds or abnormal sounds should be investigated. (See page 63.)

Skin pinch test

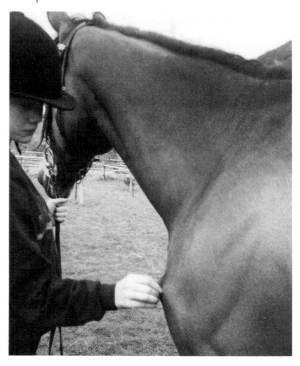

MEDICINES, ADMINISTRATION AND INJECTIONS

Medicines are substances used in the treatment of disease. These may be purchased over the counter by anyone if on the G.S.L. (general sales list), or be P.O.M. (prescription only medicine), prescribed by the veterinary surgeon to treat a specific case. P.M.L. preparations are specially listed veterinary products which may be sold by pharmacists, agricultural merchants or veterinary suppliers.

Certain guidelines should be followed before using any medication:

Check the label to make sure that you are giving the correct medicine to the correct patient. Check the dose rate, the dose interval, and the route of administration. Make sure the medicine has been correctly stored and is within the expiry date. Check it has not been contaminated with other products and that it has not altered in appearance. Read the list of contraindications for use and make sure this drug is compatible with any other treatment the patient is receiving. Some medicines are not suitable for pregnant mares, young foals or animals with liver and kidney disease. There may be competition rules that relate to the drug and a withdrawal period. Some drugs cannot be used on animals intended for meat production and although horse meat is not used for human consumption in the U.K. it is in the rest of the E.U. Follow all instructions carefully and always complete the course of treatment.

Always wash your hands before and after handling medicines. Keep a written record each time you use any medicine and dispose of empty

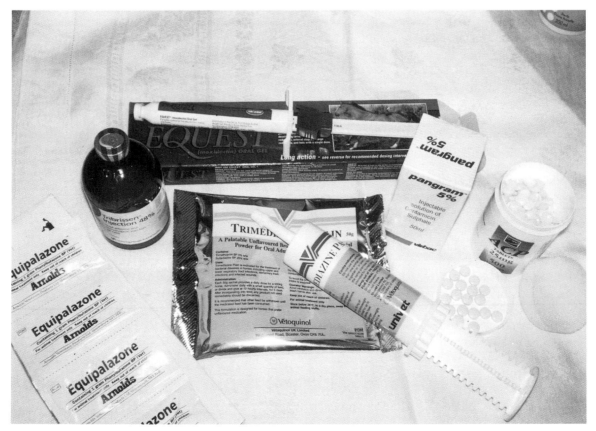

Medicines used on equines

containers and bottles in the veterinary clinical waste. Return all syringes and needles to the vet for disposal.

Medicines may be administered to the animal by a variety of methods:

Topical application

Products used to treat eye conditions and skin diseases are usually applied directly onto the affected area.

Care should be taken when applying drops or ointment to the surface of the eye to avoid further damage. Hold the nozzle parallel to the surface of the eye to prevent stabbing the eye if the horse suddenly moves its head. Animals that need frequent eye medication may become head shy and resist treatment. They will probably be fitted with a lacrimal catheter. The solution is injected into the catheter to avoid handling the horse's painful eye. Care must be taken to prevent contaminating nozzles on tubes of ointment and cream.

Skin preparations such as insecticides are often pour-on formulations. The amount needed is calculated on body-weight and poured down the dorsal midline from the poll to the dock. Washes used to treat fungal and bacterial infections may be concentrated powders or liquids which need to be diluted to the correct concentration before use. Some are left to dry on the coat and others may be rinsed off after a certain time. It may be necessary to clip off a thick coat so that the medicine can be applied to the skin.

Systemic medicines

These include oral and injectable preparations.

Oral products may be powders, pills, pastes or liquids. They may be mixed in the animal's food and the smell and taste concealed by adding treacle, peppermint oil or garlic powder. This method cannot be used on animals with a poor appetite or if you are encouraging them to eat. Good eaters may be put off their food after being offered medicated feeds. The horse has to be watched until it has eaten the complete feed which is time consuming. Pills can easily be lost in a feed so it is safer to feed by hand; push them into the flesh of a ripe pear or apple or fondant mint. Small quantities of powder can be mixed with fruit juice or treacle and spread onto bread; the sandwich is hand fed.

Pastes can be given in a dosing syringe. The animal's mouth must be empty before dosing with the paste. Stand by the horse's right shoulder facing the same direction as the horse. Cradle the head in the left arm with the palm of the hand on the nose above the nostrils. Hold the dosing syringe with the calibrated amount of medicine in the right hand. Place the nozzle of the syringe in the corner of the horse's mouth pointing towards the back of the tongue. Press the plunger to deposit the paste as far back as possible in the mouth. Keep the head up until it has swallowed. (See page 18.)

Small volumes of liquid may be mixed in a feed or made into a paste and squirted into the mouth. Large volumes of liquid should be administered via a nasogastric tube. It is dangerous to drench fluids as they may accidentally be poured into the trachea and cause respiratory problems, e.g. inhalation pneumonia.

Injectable medication

Many equine medicines are only available in an injectable form. The same considerations apply when using injectables as other medicines. Adverse or allergic reactions may occur with any medicine but probably the signs are seen more rapidly with an injectable drug.

The medicine will be injected into the muscle or a vein or under the skin. Each product should be injected into the correct tissue so that it is correctly absorbed and will not cause a reaction at the injection site. The route of injection will be stated on the label.

Injectable preparations are in single or multi-dose bottles. Horse vaccines tend to be packaged in individual syringes or single dose bottles. Special care is needed when using multidose bottles to prevent contamination of the remaining medicine.

The rubber cap should be cleaned with surgical spirit before and after use. Partly used bottles should be kept in a clean, cool, dark, dry and locked cupboard, preferably in a sealed box, not on a dusty window ledge! They should only be used if the contents are sterile and to treat the animal they were prescribed for. Syringes, needles and catheters are sterilised and individually packaged ready for use and should not be reused.

The size of syringe is determined by the volume of drug to be used. Large volumes may be injected into more than one site. When large amounts of fluid or irritant fluids

Syringes and needles commonly used on equines

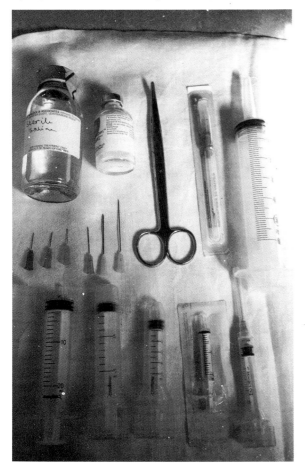

are given intravenously a catheter is used instead of a needle. The gauge of the needle/catheter has to be wide enough to allow the drug through easily and quickly. The thicker the liquid the wider the needle. The needle length is chosen to suit the injection site and size of the animal. Used needles and syringes should be replaced in the containers and returned to the vet to be disposed of in the clinical waste.

Medicines are categorised according to their action on specific tissues or organs, e.g. analgesics, sedatives and anaesthetics act on the central nervous system. Anthelmintics, antifungal drugs and antibiotics are all used to treat different infective agents, i.e., worms, fungi and bacteria. The label will have the brand name and the name of the pharmacological active ingredient and the preservative and any carrier or suspension material. The amount of active ingredient in units per ml is also stated so that an accurate dose can be calculated to treat a specific condition. When using different brands of the same ingredient always check that they contain the same concentration of active ingredient to avoid over- or under-dosing the patient.

Injection techniques

Treatments to be administered by injection are either into a vein (intravenous, I/V), into a muscle (intramuscular, I/M), or under the skin (subcutaneous, S/C). Intravenous injections are performed by the vet, usually into the jugular vein in the neck. Subcutaneous injections are placed where the skin is loosely attached to the underlying tissue, e.g. in front of the shoulder. I/M injections are the most common route used and often nurses, lay staff and owners are trained to perform these injections. Intramuscular injections may be given into any of the large muscle masses; usually the neck, the rump and thigh or the brisket are chosen sites. It is necessary to know the anatomy of the area to be injected and the landmarks used to find the correct location to insert the needle. It is important that the

Fig.38. Landmarks for intramuscular injection sites in the neck and rump

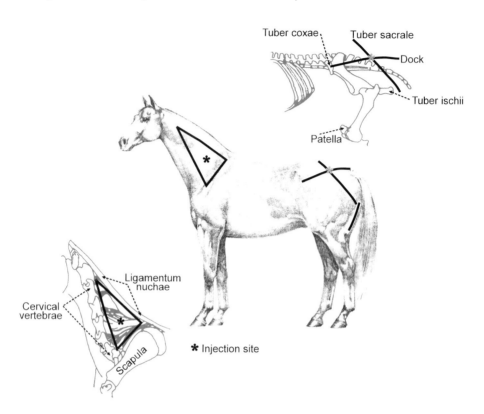

medicine is injected into the muscle mass and not into a blood vessel or fat tissue, connective tissue, ligament etc. (See photograph, page 11).

There are advantages and disadvantages to all these sites. The injection site is chosen on personal preference, the volume and nature of drug to be injected, the age, size and temperament of animal.

1. The neck

The landmarks are the cervical vertebrae, the shoulder blade and the crest/ligamentum nuchae. These structures form a triangle, bordering the injection site into the splenius muscle. The needle is inserted through the skin into the muscle about a hand's width above the shoulder blade and midway between the vertebrae and the crest. It is easy to restrain the horse for injections into the

neck muscle and the skin is thin, so it is easy to insert the needle. The muscle mass is small, so this site is unsuitable for large volumes. The horse may develop a stiff neck if the injection is sited too close to the vertebrae. The drug will be poorly absorbed if injected into the ligament or the fatty crest. Poor or dirty injection technique can result in an abscess which will require draining. This site is unsuitable for young foals or poorly muscled equines except for small volumes of 1 to 2 ml.

2. Rump

The landmarks for injecting into the gluteal muscle are where a line from the top of the croup to the point of the buttocks crosses a line from the point of the hip to the dock. The muscle mass is large and suitable for higher volume of drugs than the neck. It may be difficult to restrain some larger horses for injecting in this site. The skin is thicker so more force is needed to insert the needle and there is poor drainage if an abscess forms.

3. Thigh

The hamstring muscles, the semimembranosus and the semitendinosus are situated at the back of the leg. The thigh is the injection site of choice in foals as the muscle mass is large compared to the neck at this age. It is easier to drain an abscess at this site compared to the rump. Needles that are too long may deposit the drug close to the sciatic nerve and cause a temporary paralysis and knuckling of the foot.

4. Brisket

The pectoral muscles are easy to locate and used for small volumes of drugs. The skin is thin in this site and there will be good drainage if an abscess forms. Often the site is painful and swollen after injections because of a haematoma formation. The horse has to be adequately restrained – it must not move forwards or strike out as this makes injections at this site difficult.

Preparation of the skin site

Unless the skin area is prepared in the same way as a surgical site skin sterility is not achieved. This would mean clipping the hair and shaving the site before cleaning with an antiseptic solution. This procedure is only used for placement of catheters into veins and injections into synovial structures.

Cleaning the hair over the injection site with surgical spirit is just a token gesture that removes dirt from the hair, it does not kill bacteria on the skin.

Cleaning the area with antiseptic solutions is beneficial if the cleaning is thorough and the solution remains on the skin for a couple of minutes prior to the injection.

Horses often anticipate injections by the smell of surgical spirit or antiseptic as well as the syringe being brandished in front of them!

Most intramuscular injection sites are not sterilised. An area of skin is chosen that is not wet or muddy. The injector should wash their hands prior to selecting a sterile syringe and needle. The top of the needle container is removed and the needle attached to the syringe. If they are not properly attached the drug will spill out of the syringe or air will enter the syringe. The needle cap is left on and the medication label is checked for the drug name, dose and route of injection. The bottle is shaken to mix the contents and inverted. The syringe is then filled and the cap is removed from the needle and inserted through the clean rubber stopper on the bottle. The point of the needle should remain below the fluid level in the bottle while the plunger is withdrawn and the fluid enters the syringe. Slightly more treatment than is needed is drawn into the syringe and then the excess pushed back into the bottle. The needle is then removed from the bottle and a new, sterile needle attached to the syringe for injecting into the horse. The needle used to fill the syringe will be blunt as it has been pushed through the rubber cap on the bottle.

An assistant restrains the horse on a head collar in the stable. The horse's eye can be covered with a cupped hand so that they are unaware of the person with the syringe. They can be offered a small treat like a carrot or apple so that they are relaxed for the injection; it is much harder to inject into tense muscle. Animals that are needle-shy have had a bad injection experience; these animals should be treated sympathetically. Use a different injection site to the one normally used and do not bang the injection site before inserting the needle as this makes the horse tense the muscle. Take the animal outside on a bridle and do not swab the skin with chemicals that forewarn the horse. Use a new, sharp needle to insert through the skin. Make sure the injection fluid is not icy cold. Let the handler speak to the horse to reassure it. The actual injection technique is a matter of personal preference. Some vets bang the muscle with the back of the hand before darting in the needle and then attach the loaded syringe providing no blood is dripping from the needle. If the needle enters a blood vessel it must be repositioned. Other vets prefer to pinch a fold of skin adjacent to the injection site and thrust the needle firmly into the muscle with the syringe attached. The needle must not be allowed to move once in place as this will tear the muscle fibres. The plunger is pulled back to check that no blood enters the syringe in which case the needle is in a vessel and must be removed. When the needle is correctly placed the hub of the syringe and needle are held between finger and thumb and the plunger steadily depressed. The needle is then withdrawn and the cap replaced to avoid accidentally stabbing anyone else.

Sometimes a small amount of blood is seen at the injection site; this should be cleaned.

Different sites or sides of the animal should be used if they are receiving a course of injections. The injection sites should be checked for heat, pain, swelling or abscessation. Animals with stiff necks may be unable to reach food or water. Analgesics may be given to reduce the inflammation and pain.

Some animals develop an allergic or adverse reaction to the drug. This may be because it was injected into the wrong site by mistake. Serious reactions usually occur within a few minutes of the injection and need prompt treatment by the vet.

Occasionally needles are dropped on to the floor and have to be found and destroyed. Needles may break, especially if the horse is struggling. These have to be removed by the vet.

There should be no problems following an I/M injection providing the horse co-operates and a good sterile technique is used. Syringes may be cleaned and resterilised but needles are always destroyed.

First Aid

When presented with a sick or injured animal it may be necessary to perform first aid to prevent the condition deteriorating and to improve the chance of recovery. Although most first aid carried out is not life-saving it can make a difference to the prognosis. First aid should improve the prognosis, not make the situation worse. An example of this would be using concentrated antiseptics on a trivial wound and causing a chemical dermatitis. The overuse of poultices is another example of enthusiastic first aid. If it is not broken don't fix it. It is sometimes better to do nothing rather than do the wrong thing. It is far more constructive to seek professional advice as soon as possible. All stables should have a first aid kit in the tack room and probably a second kit for use when travelling. It is also recommended to carry a small kit when hacking. The veterinary surgeon for the premises will advise on first aid equipment. Contents of a first aid kit may include the following items:

Clinical thermometer
Jar of Vaseline
Scissors (round ended, half curved) to clip hair from wounds and cut dressings to size.
Rechargeable electric clippers.
Soap or bacterial hand wash and a towel or kitchen roll.
Plastic measuring jug for accurately diluting irrigating fluid and antiseptic solutions.
Plastic bowl or tray for carrying dressing materials.
Surgical gloves.
Plastic bags for clinical waste and to cover foot dressings.
Twitch.
Surgical boot to fit over the bandaged foot, e.g. barrier boot.
Disposable nappies (these make good foot dressings).
Salt to make a saline solution to irrigate wounds.
Plastic plant spray or a Mills wound irrigator.
Antiseptics, e.g. Pevidine or Hibiscrub.
Cotton wool 1 × 500 roll.
Roll gamgee tissue.
Cool pack.
Opsite wound spray (permeable plastic skin) for clean trivial wounds.
Poultice, e.g. Animalintex to use on the foot.
Intrasite gel; apply directly onto cleansed wounds.

Wound dressing materials

There are many products that use the moist wound healing system. The kit should contain various sizes of dressings, e.g. 5 cm × 5 cm, 10 cm × 10 cm, 10 cm × 20 cm in the following types:

These may be non-adherent, i.e. do not stick to the wound; non-adhesive, i.e. do not stick to the surrounding hair or skin; absorbent, i.e. absorb wound exudate. There are dressings that encourage debridement, i.e. removal of dead tissue, and promote granulation of tissue.

1 Non-adhesive, non-adherent absorbent dressing, e.g. Allevyn.
2 Non-adhesive, absorbent dressing, e.g. Melolin.
3 Antiseptic dressing, e.g. Inadine with Pevidine or Activate with carbon.
4 Paraffin gauze, a fine mesh impregnated with paraffin.
   Impregnated gauze, an open mesh coated with antibiotic ointment.
5 Kaltostat, a seaweed based dressing that reduces haemorrhage and is incorporated into the wound.

Bandages

Bandages suitable for horses should be 7½ cm or 10 cm wide and 2 to 3 m long.

There are many designs of bandages on the market; they may conform to the limb; they may stick to themselves but not the animal, i.e. cohesive; they may stretch or be elasticated.

1 Polyester orthopaedic padding, a soft bandage that can be used to hold the dressings in place, e.g. Ortho band, Soffban plus.
2 Non-adhesive, stretch, cohesive, conforming bandages, e.g. Vetrap, Co-Plus, Equiwrap.
3 White open weave cotton; these are cheap and strong but non-conforming, non-cohesive and non-stretch.
4 Crepe bandages are washable, easy to use, stretch and conform but are not cohesive.
5 Conforming stretch bandages, e.g. K-BAND or Knit-Firm.
6 Adhesive tape to secure bandages, e.g. surgical tape, zinc oxide tape or insulating tape.

7 Elasticated adhesive tape, e.g. Elastoplast E-BAND, Treplast.
8 Stockinette; elasticated, tubular, conforming bandages useful for knees and hocks and under plaster casts, e.g. Tubigrip, Setonet.

The first aid kit should be kept in a clean container or in a cupboard and checked regularly. Used items should be replaced. It is useful to have a rechargeable torch, wire cutters, a thermos flask and a clean bucket available. The following items can also be kept with the kit:

Controller head collar and lunge line
Exercise and stable bandages
Note-pad and pen
Healthy TPR values for each horse
The vet's and farrier's phone numbers
Contact numbers for all the horse owners on the yard.

First aid kit for travelling should be kept in the vehicle with an adequate amount of water for any weather condition. It should also include:

Thermometer and stethoscope to monitor temperature and heart-rate, to detect heat stress, dehydration and exhaustion.
Aqua spray, an aerosol of sterile saline, or a saline pack.
Antiseptic solution with a large syringe for flushing wounds.
Commercial cool packs or a thermos for ice or a fridge with frozen peas or ice in polystyrene cups.
Curved scissors and tweezers.
Cotton wool or gamgee.
Intrasite gel.
Wound dressings and assorted bandages.
Disposable nappies.
Insect repellent.
Travelling rug, tail bandage, travel boots and poll guard.
Twitch and lunge line.
Hoof pick and barrier boot.
Two 60 cm lengths of wood to make splints.
Mobile phone.

More accidents occur while loading and unloading horses than while actually in transit. Care must be taken if the horse has to be unloaded on a busy road. It is safer to ask the police to stop all traffic and to attach a lunge line to the horse's headcollar or bridle before unloading. Accidents may occur at a sporting venue but hopefully there will be a vet in attendance.

A first aid kit to take out when hacking should fit into a standard size bum bag. It is always advisable to leave directions of your route and your probable time of return at home with a responsible person. Take the following items:

* Money/phone card/mobile phone. Vet's phone number.
* Plastic bag to hold all items. (This could be used on a foot or as a glove.)
* Intrasite gel.
* Allevyn adhesive dressing.
* Soffban and Vetrap bandage.
* Space blanket.
* Plastic waterbottle.

If the horse is injured, dismount immediately and keep the horse as still as possible until you have assessed the extent of the injury. Sudden lameness may be caused by a foot injury, a soft tissue injury to a tendon, ligament or muscle or a bone injury such as a fracture or dislocation. If the condition is serious, get help immediately and do not move the horse. Try to keep calm and avoid exciting the horse with unnecessary movement by other people or horses. Do not put anyone in a dangerous situation. Restrain the horse as quietly as possible and try to reassure it while help is on the way. If the horse can move easily it can be moved from a road to a safer place to wait for help.

Practical wound management

First aid for wounds:

1 Assess the size, depth, site and type.
The wound may be a simple skin wound, a bruise, graze, incised or lacerated wound. It may be a complicated wound with arterial bleeding or involve tendons or synovial structures or body cavities. Some small puncture wounds have very serious consequences if they involve a joint or a tendon sheath. The tetanus vaccination status of the horse should be checked. It may be decided at this point that assistance is needed.

2 Control the bleeding.

Keep the horse still to stop the blood pressure rising. Arterial bleeding is bright red and squirts out in pulses. A clean cloth or pad is placed directly over the bleeding and held or bandaged into place. Apply direct pressure over the site for at least 10 to 15 minutes. Place second and third dressings with bandages over the site if the bleeding seeps through the first bandage. If the bleeding cannot be controlled seek assistance immediately.

Venous bleeding is dark red or purple and runs out in a steady stream. It will usually clot if covered with a dressing and firm bandage.

Capillary bleeding oozes from the wound and will normally clot.

3 Prevent further damage.

Restrain the horse. Movement increases bleeding and opens the wound edges. Avoid further contamination of the wound. Apply a non-adherent dressing and a bandage to provide support, pressure, and prevent contamination.

Assistance may now be sought.

4 Clean the wound.

Wounds that are simple and not grossly contaminated or bleeding badly may be cleaned.

Antiseptics must be used at the correct dilution otherwise they kill living cells.

Water pressure from hose pipes is too strong to use on wounds. The water forces debris into the depths of the wound and totally waterlogs the tissues so delaying the healing process.

The wound can be flushed with sterile saline solution using a 60 ml syringe with an 18 gauge needle attached; a hand-held plastic indoor plant sprayer; a Mills wound irrigator or an Aquaspray aerosol.

A saline solution is made by adding a teaspoonful of salt to a pint of previously boiled water.

The hair from the skin edges should be removed to allow full inspection of the wound. The wound is filled with intrasite gel or K-Y GEL to prevent the cut hair falling into the wound.

The wound is then irrigated again with saline solution.

The wound is dressed according to the type and status.

First aid treatment for specific types of wound:

1 *Bruise*

Rinse with saline.

Dry on a paper towel.

Apply a cool pack over a sheet of gamgee or wool to control the bleeding for 30 minutes.

Call the vet if the area is very painful or the horse is lame.

2 *Abrasion*

Wash with saline to remove surface contamination.

Apply cool pack over a non-adherent dressing for 30 minutes.

Apply Intrasite gel, Allevyn and bandage to give support.

Call the vet if there is pain, swelling or lameness.

3 *Incised wounds*

Control the bleeding with a pressure pad and bandage.

If the bleeding is not serious clean with saline.

Apply Intrasite gel, a non-adherent dressing and bandage.

Call the vet as the wound may need sutures.

4 *Lacerated wounds*

These wounds always require veterinary attention.

Clean with saline to remove gross contamination.

Apply Intrasite gel, Allevyn dressing and bandage to support and protect limb wounds while waiting for the vet.

Large wounds on the body can be protected with a clean tablecloth, pillow case or cotton sheet. The vet will be required if the wound is to be sutured or if it is grossly contaminated or already infected or if it is a complicated wound.

5 *Contaminated wounds*

Irrigate with warm saline solution providing there is no bleeding.

Dress and bandage to prevent further contamination.

6 *Infected wounds*

Flush with warm saline to remove pus and exudate.

Dress and bandage.

7 *Complicated wounds*

Do not move the horse.

Do not wash the wound.

Apply Intrasite gel, Allevyn dressing and a firm bandage.

A Robert Jones bandage or splints may be needed before the horse can be moved if it has a serious tendon, joint or bone injury.

The horse may be in shock and should be kept warm. A thermatex rug may be placed over the cotton sheet if there is an injury to the chest or abdomen.

Dressings are normally held in place by bandages on limb wounds. All the necessary materials to treat the wound should be prepared before the horse is restrained. Packets should be opened and cotton wool or gamgee cut to size before the treatment commences. The vet may advise on which dressing is to be used at each stage of healing depending on the amount of exudate and sepsis. The frequency at which the bandages are changed should also be under veterinary supervision. Clean wounds with little exudate may need to be redressed every three or four days whereas heavily contaminated wounds may need to be redressed every twelve to twenty-four hours.

Reasons for applying bandages

Bandages are used to hold wound dressings and catheters in place. They protect wounds from contamination with faeces and trauma from bedding materials and prevent the animal licking or biting the wound. Bandages can help control haemorrhage and swelling. They support injured tissue, prevent movement of wound edges and suppress the formation of granulation tissue. They reduce pain by restricting movement and reduce swelling. They also provide warmth and keep the under layers in place to distribute pressure evenly over the limb.

In all cases of injury it is best to cover a good length of the limb above and below the injury in the bandage. A distal limb injury will be bandaged from just below the carpus or tarsus to the distal pastern.

First layer
Wounds require a dressing material to absorb exudate, remove dead tissue and maintain asepsis. This is held in place by orthopaedic felt.
This layer is only required if there is a wound.

Second layer
A layer of cotton wool or gamgee applied so that it conforms to the limb and lies flat without ridges or lumps.
This is held in place by conforming, cohesive stretch bandages.

Third layer
This is the sealing layer and is either an adhesive, elasticated bandage like Elastoplast or a cohesive, stretch bandage like Vetrap.

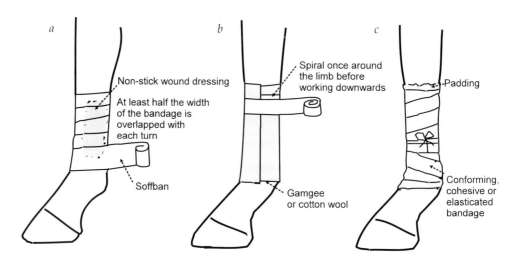

Fig.39. (a) *Bandage for a wound to the cannon.*
(b) *Applying a stable bandage over gamgee or fybegee.*
(c) *Applying a support or exercise bandage.*

Fig.40. Applying a figure-of-eight bandage to the left fore-knee.

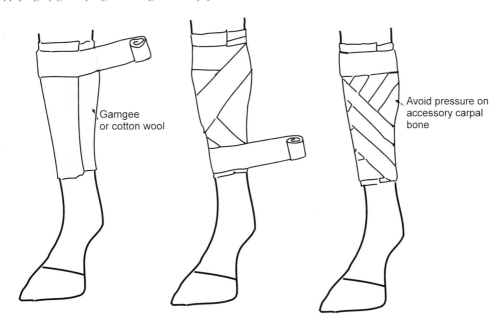

Gamgee
or cotton wool

Avoid pressure on
accessory carpal
bone

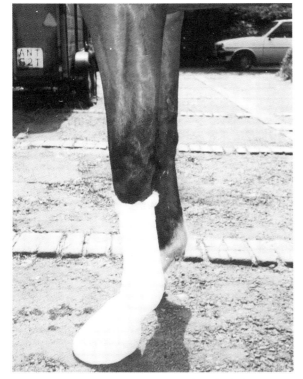

This horse had injured her pastern and heel. The lower limb was swollen to a point slightly below the knee. The foot was included in the bandage.

Bandaging limbs

Prepare all materials and ask an assistant to hold the horse. Apply a non-adherent dressing to the wound and bandage in place using orthopaedic felt. The right legs are bandaged in a clockwise direction and the left legs in an anti-clockwise direction. This pulls the flexor tendons to the inside of the limb. Each turn of the bandage overlaps the previous turn by half its width. Even pressure should be used so that the bandage is snug to the limb. A piece of gamgee or cotton wool is wrapped around the limb with the overlap on the outside and pointing backwards. A cohesive, conforming stretch bandage is used to hold the padding in place. The bandage is unwrapped and pulled to half its stretch as it is applied round the limb. Depending on the length of the bandage it may be possible to spiral down the leg and back up to the top of the dressing. Do not stretch the last 10 cm of a cohesive bandage, just press it flat against the last layer of bandage so that it will stick properly. The bandage should not overlap the padding at the top and bottom of the bandage. An adhesive elasticated bandage can be applied to

129

give extra support and protection to the injury. Do not attach adhesive bandages to the horse's skin or hair if the bandage is to be removed each day. Injuries to the fetlock or pastern should be bandaged from the hoof to just below the knee or hock.

Adhesive bandages can be attached to the hoof wall to prevent bedding material getting inside the bandage. Bandages should be comfortable, not too tight and should not fall down.

If the bandage is too tight there will be swelling above and below it. The leg will be painful to touch when the bandage is removed. Tight bandages can result in skin sloughs and areas of white hair (acquired marks). The horse may chew the bandage if there is any discomfort.

Bandages may be protected with boots or stable bandages. Support bandages may be applied to the non-affected limbs if the horse is lame and reluctant to move.

Bandaging the knee

The knee is a difficult site to bandage as gravity is against you. The top of the limb is wider than the bottom so the bandage tends to slip down the leg. The knee is constantly bending which moves the bandage. The bony prominences of the knee should not be covered with a tight bandage as it is easy to cause pressure sores on the skin over the accessory carpal bone and the medial distal radius. The bandage is unwrapped in a figure-of-eight to avoid the bony prominences. When the bandaging is complete the outer layer can be incised over the pressure points to relieve any tension caused by traction on the padding. A lower limb support bandage with padding and a stable bandage is applied, this prevents filling of the distal limb and also prevents the carpal bandage slipping down.

Bandaging the hock

The hock is bandaged in the usual three or two layer method avoiding pressure on the point of the hock. A figure-of-eight method is used which allows the horse to bend the hock without causing pressure on the point of the hock. A distal limb stable bandage is applied for the same reason as the knee.

Alternatives to bandages for knees and hocks are:

* Tubular stockinette
* Lycra stockings with zip fastenings
* Neoprene shaped support boots with adjustable velcro fastenings

These are all available in various sizes.

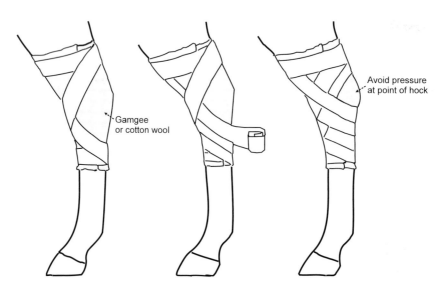

Fig.41. Bandage technique for the left hind hock; the bandage is unwrapped in an anticlockwise direction.

Tubular stockinette is cut to the required length. A small plastic bag is placed over the foot so the stocking will stay clean and be easier to slip over the foot. The stocking is rolled into a doughnut and pulled over the foot. It is taken up the limb above the area to be bandaged and rolled down to hold a dressing in place. The horse's hair should be laid flat.

The lower end of the stocking can be rolled up to clean the wound or replace the dressing. The upper end of the stocking may be secured with Elastoplast. A stable bandage is used on the lower limb.

Bandaging the foot

The foot may be enclosed in a bandage to protect the sole, the wall and injuries to the heels and coronary band. Bandages last longer if the foot is unshod. Horseshoes cut through the bandage if the horse is walking on a hard surface. Disposable nappies conform well to the foot and are easier to secure than a square of gamgee or cotton wool. A stretch, cohesive bandage anchored around the pastern and covering the foot in a figure-of-eight is applied over the nappy. This may be covered by Elastoplast or

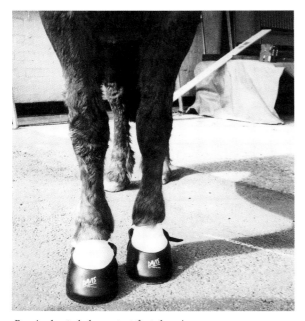

Barrier boots help protect foot dressings

waterpoof tape or a barrier boot. The foot tends to sweat if kept inside plastic bags or rubber boots and the bandages will be damp. It is important to have a high standard of stable hygiene to prevent the bandages being contaminated with faeces and urine. The bed should be thick and clean.

Poulticing the foot

Poulticing infected wounds was a popular practice and many products were used, e.g. bran and epsom salts, kaolin, magnesium sulphate paste. Today the only area poulticed is the sole of the foot and usually with the commercially prepared poultice.

Animalintex consists of a thick padding impregnated with bassorin and boric acid. The padding has a polythene backing. The poultice is cut to the required size and placed polythene side upmost in a dish of hot water. It is squeezed almost dry and the padding side placed against the cleansed foot, with a pad of gamgee or wool over it. This is covered in a foot bandage or a sock to hold the padding in place. The poultice remains warm for a short time and may improve the blood supply to that area. The polythene backing retains the heat and keeps the moisture in the padding. The poultice is supposed to draw any infection out of a hole or defect in the hoof capsule, it also softens the hoof horn and may make paring the hoof easier. The poultice is replaced at twelve hour intervals until it has had the desired effect. Overuse of poultices creates a wet, smelly foot.

Tubbing the foot

Hot tubbing is a useful method to improve the circulation to the foot and encourage abscesses to burst. The foot is cleaned and scrubbed to remove gross contamination. The horse is held by an assistant and the affected foot is lifted. The shallow bowl or bucket is positioned where you are going to place the foot. As the foot is put down the assistant picks up the opposite front leg to prevent the horse stepping out of the container. If a hind foot is being treated the front

multiple layers of cotton wool compressed by conforming bandages. It can be applied as a half or full limb bandage.

It is used to stabilise limb fractures, to restrict soft tissue damage, control limb oedema and to support wounds.

To construct an RJB four to eight rolls of cotton wool, eight to fifteen conforming bandages plus six rolls of adhesive bandage are required. Splints may be incorporated into the bandage to give more support and rigidity. This is especially useful when moving fracture patients. Not all fractures are untreatable but many become so due to incorrect first aid and damage during travelling and movement of the horse.

Applying an RJB

Wounds are cleaned and covered in a non-adherent sterile dressing held in place by orthopaedic felt. Cotton wool is applied snugly around the leg from the foot to the knee or hock for a half

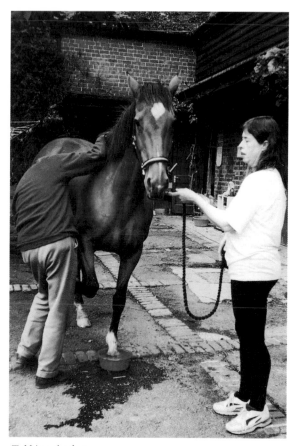

Tubbing the foot

limb on the same side should be lifted. A hand is placed on the front of the knee or cannon bone to keep the foot in the bowl. Warm water is slowly added to the bowl until the hoof is submerged, more water may be added as the water cools. Sometimes the water is added to the container before the horse's foot is placed in it, but it is often kicked over or spilled before the horse is positioned. Tubbing the foot may be repeated several times during the day. The limb is dried carefully between sessions. This method is cheap and easy and avoids using so many expensive bandages.

The Robert Jones bandage

A Robert Jones bandage (RJB) is constructed with many layers and uses a large amount of dressing material. It is strong and rigid due to the

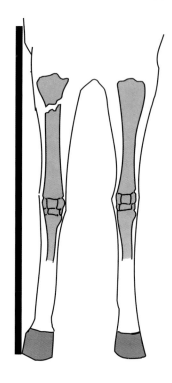

Fig.42. A lateral splint from the ground to the shoulder is used to stabilise a fracture of the radius.

Fig.43. The foreleg divided into four regions for Robert Jones bandaging and splinting.

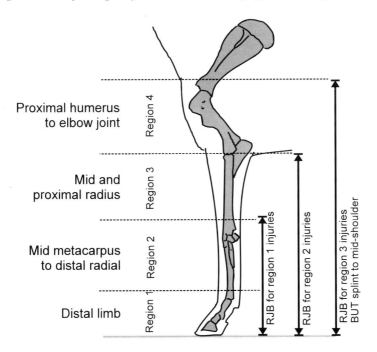

Proximal humerus
to elbow joint   Region 4

Mid and
proximal radius   Region 3

Mid metacarpus
to distal radial   Region 2

Distal limb   Region 1

RJB for region 1 injuries

RJB for region 2 injuries

RJB for region 3 injuries
BUT splint to mid-shoulder

limb or to the elbow or stifle for the full limb. Each layer should be 2 to 3 cm thick. Conforming bandages are used to compress the cotton wool using firm pressure so that the bandaged limb is a uniform thickness. This means that more wool is placed around the narrower areas of the leg, e.g. the pastern. A second cotton wool layer of 2 or 3 cm is wrapped around the limb and compressed with conforming bandages. This is repeated for at least three layers. Each layer should be evened out with half width wool on any narrow places. When all the layers have been applied the entire bandage is wrapped in elastic adhesive bandage maintaining an even pressure throughout. The finished RJB should look like a cylinder.

Splints are added to support fractures or where the suspensory apparatus is damaged and when a full limb RJB has been applied. Splints may be wooden or plastic guttering. The ends of the splints should be covered in padding to prevent them traumatising the skin. Wooden splints should be approximately 53 and 84 cm (21 and 33 in) long by $2^{1}/_{2} \times 5$ cm (1×2 in) depending on

the size of the horse and the area to be splinted. Guttering should be used in a double layer. The splints are attached to the RJB by heavy duty tape.

The fore and hindlimb may be divided into four regions which require different splinting techniques.

REGION 1
Injuries from the distal cannon to the foot require an RJB from the ground surface of the hoof wall to the knee or hock. The bones should be aligned before applying the splint to the front of the limb. The foreleg is held off the ground by an assistant holding it by the forearm so that the dorsal surfaces of the distal limb bones are aligned. The hindlimb is held above the hock to align the distal bones.

REGION 2
Injuries between the distal radius and the mid-cannon in the forelimb require an RJB from the ground to the elbow, with splints on the outside and back surface of the bandage.

Fig.44. The hindleg divided into four regions for Robert Jones bandaging and splinting.

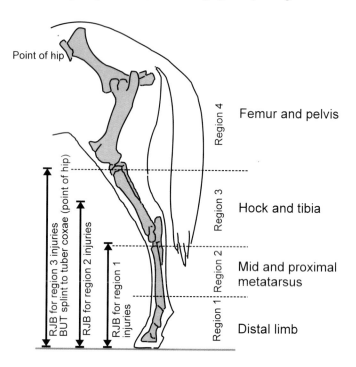

Injuries between the top and mid-section of the hind cannon require a full limb RJB with splints to the height of the hock on the outside and back of the limb.

REGION 3

Injuries to the radius require a full limb RJB with splints on the lateral side of the limb from ground to mid-shoulder. Injuries to the tibia or hock should have a full limb RJB with a splint from the ground to the hip on the lateral side of the limb.

REGION 4

Fractures to the ulna, humerus and scapula cannot be splinted. If the knee is fixed with a splint over padding to the back of the limb from the fetlock to the elbow the horse will move more easily.

Hindlimb fractures to region 4 cannot be splinted. Horses with heavily splinted and bandaged limbs may move awkwardly or panic, so the utmost care must be taken when moving them to prevent injury to the handlers.

TRANSPORTING INJURED EQUINES

The legal situation

There are a number of rules relating to the transport of injured and sick animals in the Welfare of Animals During Transport Order 1992 that apply to equines:

* No animal may be transported in a manner that causes, or is likely to cause it injury or unnecessary suffering.
* No person shall cause or allow the transport of an animal that is unfit to travel because it is diseased, infirm, ill, injured, newborn or given birth within the last 48 hours or likely to give birth in transit except under veterinary guidance.
* Only a veterinary surgeon is qualified to decide if an equine can be transported and it can only be moved to the nearest hospital which has the expertise, equipment and personnel needed to treat it. It can only be moved in the presence of and under the supervision of the vet.

Type of vehicle

Injured horses are transported in specially designed horse ambulances or in a standard horse box or horse trailer.

* Horse ambulances.
  These are mandatory on racecourses and available at many competition venues. They are supplied with experienced drivers and horse handlers. If competitors insisted on this facility at all shows with a duty equine veterinary surgeon on site, the treatment and movement of injured animals would improve.
  Trailer ambulances should be towed by a four wheel drive vehicle. They must have low loading front and rear ramps with a shallow slope. The internal partitions must be well padded and easily moved. There should be a drag mat and a winch for moving recumbent or unconscious animals. A belly sling is used to support animals that are likely to go down or are unsteady on their feet. The person travelling with the patient should be able to reach all sides of the animal with ease. There should be good internal lighting.
  Obviously ambulances must be well maintained with good suspension to give a smooth ride. They should be well ventilated with plenty of headroom inside and in the doorways. The handler

should be able to communicate with the driver during the journey.
* Regular horse box and trailer.
  Ordinary transport vehicles may be used to travel the injured horse providing the ramps are low and gently sloping and there is adequate space inside with narrow partitions for the horse to lean against. The space between partitions may be reduced with mattresses or duvet covers filled with straw tied to the partition. Bales of straw may be used under the horse instead of a belly band. The floor of the vehicle should be checked to make sure that it will support the horse with extra weight on the sound limb, if not, it should be reinforced with thick plywood. The partitions must be easy to move for unloading and if the horse falls down in transit. Before loading the horse it is important to consider where it is to be unloaded and whether the ramps can be positioned to unload at the correct side. Do not load an animal into a trailer if it cannot be unloaded at the end of the journey!

The veterinary surgeon will examine the horse and apply bandages and splints and administer analgesics etc. before it is moved. The trailer should be positioned near the horse on level, smooth ground if possible. The material on the ramp and floor should be non-slip like shavings, sand or rubber mats. Ideally the horse should travel with the injured limb to the rear of the vehicle, this is only possible if there are forward and rear ramps to allow easy unloading. The horse should be held on a bridle and allowed to walk a few steps on the flat to adjust to the splints and RJB. Well supported horses can walk quite well on three legs if moved quietly and carefully.

A sensible, calm person should travel with the horse. The horse must be allowed to use its head and neck to balance itself during transit. The bar in front of and behind the horse should be padded to restrict movement and allow the horse to lean against it. The driver must be considerate and take the route with the least bends, hills and traffic lights etc. A long journey is not ideal as the horse will become exhausted. There is a list of hospitals, with the facilities needed, that are willing to take emergency cases, see page 150. They should be informed in advance that the patient is en route and the estimated time of arrival. The veterinary surgeon who has been treating the horse should send written details of the treatment to date and speak to the hospital duty vet.

The Blue Cross horse ambulance (The Blue Cross)

The interior of the ambulance is fitted with adjustable supports and slings (The Blue Cross)

Nursing Sick Horses

General considerations

Horses may be nursed on the owners' premises or in a hospital facility. Stables used to hospitalise horses should be the correct size to accommodate the patients. The floor and walls should be easy to clean. The ideal is roughened concrete floors with sealed rubber mats and cemented walls painted in water resistant paint. The stable fittings should be easily removable. The box must be well ventilated and light with wide doors that open outwards, or be on runners and move sideways. The ceiling beams must be able to support equipment to sling a horse and be the correct height. There should be easy access to pasture or a menage, as well as for vehicles to load and unload horses. The bedding material used must suit the particular patient. Disposal of stable waste must be arranged.

Isolation box

A separate stable is needed as an isolation facility for horses with infectious or contagious diseases, e.g. viral or bacterial respiratory diseases; bowel diseases like Salmonella and rotavirus; fungal skin disease, e.g. ringworm.

Ideally the isolation area should be at least 35 m and downwind from other animal housing and have separate drains. It should be situated well away from the main buildings and thoroughfares. The isolation box should have its own feed and bedding store, and equipment for mucking out. At the box entrance a disinfectant foot bath and washing facilities for the nurse are needed. The nurse should be provided with rubber footwear, waterproof, washable outer clothing and plastic disposable gloves. One person should tend to the sick horse. They should change all their clothing and shower before going near any other horses.

All waste feed and bedding material should be burned if possible. The area should be cleaned twice a day and disinfected after the patient has recovered.

All the bedding material is removed from the box before it is steam cleaned and disinfected. The area outside the box must also be disinfected.

FAM, an iodophor disinfectant and detergent steriliser is highly effective against all bacteria and most viruses. It is active in the presence of organic material and is biodegradable and relatively non-irritant and non-toxic.

Nursing patients with respiratory disease

The patient should be kept warm in a well ventilated stable. Thermatex rugs and stable bandages may be used.

Discharges from the nose and eyes may be removed with damp cotton wool, and a smear of Vaseline placed under the eyes and on the nose to prevent further discharge from sticking to the skin. The used cotton wool is placed in a polythene bag for disposal. Fresh, clean water should be easily available and replaced several times each day. Horses with sore throats and mouth ulcers may prefer lukewarm water.

The feed should be moist and nutritious; a forage based diet with soaked sugar beet is ideal. Small, frequent meals with grated carrots, apples and hand pulled grass can be offered.

The horse should have its own water buckets and feed mangers. These should be frequently cleaned to remove nasal discharges which will contaminate them.

The hay must be dust-free and soaked for five to thirty minutes before feeding from a floor container to encourage postural drainage. Soaking the hay washes out some of the dust and swells the mould and fungal spores so they are not inhaled as they are stuck to the hay.

Horses who have contact with spores when they have a viral respiratory infection, which damages the cells lining the tract, may later develop allergic respiratory disease, e.g. COPD. Inappetent horses can be encouraged to eat if they have their heads steamed with eucalyptus or friars balsam vapours before they are fed. These aromatic oils are placed in a steamer or a bucket on cotton wool and boiling water added. The horse inhales the steam through a mask or by holding the bucket under its nose. Take care not to scald the horse!

The horse should be kept quiet and mucking out should be done with as little movement of bedding as possible to prevent airborne dust particles. Dust free white shavings or paper bedding on top of rubber mats are the best beddings. Dust extracted straw is available prepacked in bags.

Deep litter beds should be avoided as the ammonia in urine is an irritant to the respiratory tract.

The nurse should monitor progress and keep a daily record of TPR, faeces, urine and the amount the horse is eating and drinking. The medicine should be administered as advised by the vet. Medication may be given twice daily (bid) that is every 12 hours or three times daily (tid) every eight hours or four times daily (qid), every six hours. Some medicines are administered as aerosols using a nebuliser system with a face mask so the drug is inhaled into the lungs. Probiotics may be fed after antibiotic therapy.

When the patient is recovering it will accept more grooming and handling. It may be grazed in hand away from other horses or walked out to improve its mental well being. It takes four to six weeks for the respiratory tract to heal after a viral infection and during this time the horse should be convalescing.

Nursing a horse with a painful eye

Eye infections and injuries are painful and the horse may rapidly become head shy. It should be placed in a darkened box and contact with dust and flies should be avoided. Hay should be soaked and fed in a floor container, and the horse may be allowed to graze at night.

Usually a nasolacrimal catheter is fitted to administer medicaments to the eye in the acute stage of the disease. The catheter is placed into the nasal ostium in the nose and threaded up the duct. It is either sutured or glued to the external nostril and the horse's forehead and neck. It is threaded over the poll onto the opposite side of the neck to the painful eye. A head and neck cover can be worn to prevent the catheter being caught on stable fittings.

The horse should be held by an assistant standing on the horse's good side. The nurse can remove the cap on the catheter, attach the syringe to the catheter and flush solutions into the eye. The cap is cleaned and replaced. The horse may also need systemic analgesics and antibiotics.

Eye ointments are easier to apply if they are warm. Discharges are wiped away with cotton wool damped in warm boiled water. The nurse should wash her hands and wear surgical gloves. The lower eyelid is pulled away from the eyeball. The cap is removed from the tube and the hand holding the tube is rested against the horse's cheek to prevent accidentally stabbing the eye if the horse moves. The tube is held parallel to the eyeball and the ointment squeezed into the everted lid. The nozzle should be cleaned and the cap replaced. Opened tubes should be thrown away after a month. Each patient should have their own tube labelled with their name.

Nursing the colic case

All colic cases should be fitted with a padded headcollar and a pollguard. The bedding should be inedible and banked to prevent the horse becoming cast. All removable stable fittings should be taken out of the stable. The horse should not be allowed food or water unless directed by the vet. The patient should be carefully monitored without putting anyone at risk. A written record of all observations should be made and may be used by the vet to assess if the case is surgical:

* assessment of pain, both the degree and length of bouts of pain.
* heart-rate increases and continually high rates are important.
* strength of the pulse; a decrease indicates shock.

* mucous membrane and capillary refill used to monitor shock and toxaemia.
* muscle tremors usually a serious sign.
* temperature and respiratory rate.
* skin pinch to monitor dehydration.
* depression is usually a serious sign.
* gut sounds, reduction or lack of sounds in all quadrants is significant.
* passing faeces, gas and urine. The amount, colour and consistency are noted.
* digital pulses may be present in toxic animals.

The same parameters will be monitored in cases recovering from medical colics. Food and water will be given as instructed by the vet.

Surgical colics will be hospitalised after surgery and receive intensive post operative care by trained nursing staff and the veterinary team. There can be a variety of post-operative complications in these toxic and shocked patients.

When the horse has recovered to the point of eating small mashes and grass the owner may be involved with the aftercare. This involves grooming and frequent walks to encourage the horse. The owner can also monitor the physical progress and the improvement of the animal's mental attitude at this stage.

Owners often assist with the nursing of grass sickness cases. The horse's demeanour improves when visited by familiar persons and this stimulation will help to keep the horse interested. These horses may be fed by hand to encourage them to eat. The feed must be easy to swallow and nutritious especially high in protein and energy, e.g. Baileys no. 1 (high energy mash) and Alfa A (high protein forage). Succulents like freshly pulled grass, grated carrot and apples are eaten by some animals. It is a case of trying different foods to see which the horse will accept. Soaked sugar beet pulp can be used to damp grain and make it easier to swallow. Some animals prefer warm feed and lukewarm water. The appetite may vary from day to day. Frequent small feeds should be offered.

The horse should be taken for short walks and allowed to graze in hand. This will stimulate gut motility and the animal's interest. The horse may have a low body temperature and should be rugged. Thermatex rugs are the rug of choice as they are warm and allow sweat to evaporate. The horse will need to be groomed twice a day to prevent the coat becoming scurfy and sticky. The nostrils and eyes should be bathed to remove discharges and the area smeared with Vaseline. Steaming the head will encourage clearance of the nasal passages.

With good nursing about 40% of chronic grass sickness cases recover.

Nursing the recumbent horse

Horses may be recumbent for many reasons:

1 Paralysis. This may involve all four legs (quadriplegic) hindlegs (paraplegic) or both front and hindlegs on the same side (hemiplegic). This is due to loss of motor neurone function
2 Paresis or ataxia, i.e. a muscle weakness and inco-ordination
3 Prolonged recovery from anaesthesia
4 Acute infection, e.g. equine herpes infection, tetanus
5 Injuries, e.g. fracture of a limb or pelvis
6 Laminitis/acute founder/sinkers
7 Exertional myopathy
8 Unconsciousness/heart attack/stroke
9 Arthritis
10 Generalised debility/emaciation.

Owners may have to assist in nursing recumbent animals that have acute infections, injuries or laminitis. Recumbent animals are unable to get up and may not be able to move themselves onto their brisket (sternal recumbency). They will not be able to keep themselves clean or easily move towards food or water. They should be managed in a stable whenever possible. The stable must be large enough to allow the nurse and vet to work around the horse and turn the horse without risk of injury to themselves. A stable which has a high ceiling and strong beams to support a hoist is ideal.

The best bedding material is white dust-free shavings. The bed should be 45 cm (18 in) thick with deep banks. This will not move under the horse like straw and paper. Sandbags and cushions can be used to support the horse on its brisket so that it can eat and drink.

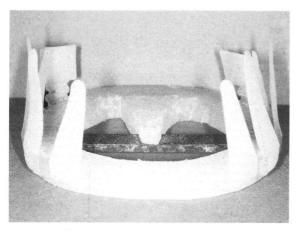

An adjustable heart bar shoe (R. A. Eustace)

Faeces and urine should be removed from the bed as soon as it is passed. Some animals will need a urinary catheter if they are incontinent or unable to pass urine.

The diet must be compatible with the patient's illness and avoid constipation. Sloppy feeds containing soaked sugar beet shreds and a nutritious high fibre diet, e.g. Alfa A or HiFi often form the bulk of the feed. The feed bucket/water bucket should be shallow with no handles. The horse may be hand fed and water offered every couple of hours when the horse is turned over. The horse's tail can be bandaged and plaited to keep it clean. The dock should be washed and dried each day.

Leg bandages will protect the limbs from rubs and a rug will protect the body. A padded headcollar and poll guard will protect the head. These should be removed twice daily and the animal massaged and groomed.

The eyes and nostrils tend to become caked in the bedding material and should be frequently cleaned. A large sheet or Vet bed can be placed under the head and neck to prevent the bedding material getting into the eyes and nostrils.

The bony prominences should be checked for bed sores (decubital sores), the areas most likely to be affected are: the point of the hip, elbow and shoulder; lateral and medial aspect of the knee, hock and fetlocks; bony ridge above the eye.

These sores must be cleaned, creamed and covered to prevent the bedding sticking to them.

The horse will be monitored in the normal way with all findings recorded and medication administered as directed by the vet. Laminitic animals will need their feet carefully checked twice daily and adjustments made to the grub-screw in the glue on adjustable heart bar shoes.

Nursing the fracture/acutely lame patient

Horses that are acutely lame need similar nursing to recumbent animals as they too will not be able to move easily.

Animals that have plaster casts/fracture surgery will require careful nursing. Bandages and casts must be checked for signs of rubs, pain or swelling. The cast must be inspected for cracks or areas of weakness. Signs of discomfort, unpleasant odour or discolouration of the cast points to a problem and it should be investigated. Signs of an increase in pain or depression should be closely monitored and the veterinary surgeon alerted to any change.

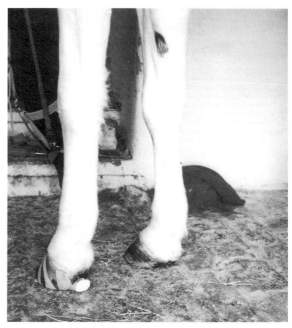

A frog support made from a roll of bandage taped to the frog

Exercise on a prepared surface

The horse will need support bandages on the other limbs and possibly frog supports. It should be rugged up as it will not be moving about. (See page 140.)

Box rest

Horses that are box rested need their body-weight and condition score checked each week to avoid wide fluctuations in body-weight. The diet should include good quality forage with a vitamin and mineral supplement.

The bedding should be kept clean to avoid respiratory and foot problems. The horse should have its feet picked out twice daily and trimmed regularly by the farrier.

Most horses adapt well to confinement in the stable while they are on box rest. The owner often does not, and is tempted to take the horse out, damaging all the surgery and veterinary treatment! As the horse recovers it will be placed on a strict exercise regime with walking in hand for set periods of time each day. Massage and physiotherapy will prevent muscle wastage and keep the horse's body toned.

The horse may be exercised in hand on a prepared surface before ridden exercise commences. Swimming and treadmill exercise may be part of the rehabilitation and fittening programme. Physiotherapy is used after injuries to enhance the body's natural repair mechanisms and restore normal function to the injured tissues.

Chartered physiotherapists working with animals should have post graduate training with veterinary surgeons and be members of the Association of Chartered Physiotherapists in Animal Therapy (ACPAT).

They are bound by a code of professional con-

duct agreed by the RCVS and the CSP. They have to work within the confines of the Veterinary Act and under the guidance of the veterinary surgeon who has diagnosed the condition that is being treated.

Physiotherapists work with animals in the rehabilitation stage of their recovery as well as the healing stage.

Therapeutic machines are used during the healing stage of injury. These act at cellular level to enhance the natural healing ability of the body. They include electrical and mechanical stimulation. These therapies often reduce swelling and give pain relief. Incorrect use of these machines can be very harmful and they should only be used on horses by members of ACPAT.

1 Magnetic field therapy, e.g. pulsing electromagnetic fields.
2. Faradic treatment, e.g. electro- muscle stimulation.
3 Therapeutic ultrasound.
4 Low level laser treatment.
5 Electrostimulation, e.g. transcutaneous electrical nerve stimulation (TENS).
6 Massage.
7 Acupuncture, e.g. heat and electrical stimulation of acupuncture points are often used in physiotherapy.
8 Heat therapy, e.g. heat lamps and solarium; hot pads and hot poulticing; hot fomentations and hot tubbing.
9 Cold therapy, e.g. cold hosing, tubbing in ice water, cool packs, cold bandages (Bonner bandages).

Cold therapy

EUTHANASIA

Euthanasia is defined as a quiet and gentle death. Euthanasia or humane destruction is rarely discussed by horse owners yet frequently they are asked to make difficult decisions at a time of great emotion and stress. It is easier if they have considered the subject and planned ahead so that they can cope in a rational manner should they have to make a quick decision. It is an advantage to be aware of all the options available in case of an emergency when immediate euthanasia is required on humane grounds to prevent unnecessary suffering. The vet is the best person to advise on humane destruction. The welfare of the animal is their first responsibility.

In an emergency situation when the horse cannot be transported a veterinary surgeon, a knackerman or a hunt kennelman will destroy the animal on site.

In a non-emergency situation the owner has to decide whether the horse should be 'put down' at home or away.

This situation is common for elderly, infirm animals and those with chronic disease or deteriorating conditions and a poor quality of life. If the animal is insured the insurance company should be informed and may request a post mortem report. These animals may well be destroyed at home in their own familiar surroundings. This is important for any companion animals who will be less stressed if they are allowed to see the body of their companion. They appear to accept death far more easily than seeing the live horse disappearing into a lorry.

If the horse is destroyed on the home premises there must be access for collection and removal of the body unless it is to be buried. Neighbours should be informed so they are not shocked or upset.

Horses that are fit to travel may be taken to the local hunt kennels or a licensed horse slaughterhouse. The transport may need to be arranged.

The horse may be destroyed by a veterinary surgeon, knackerman, hunt kennelman, or a licensed horse slaughterman.

The owner or their agent may be asked to sign a form giving their permission for the horse to be euthanased.

Whatever method is used, it should be painless and not distress the animal. There should be a rapid loss of consciousness followed by cardiac and respiratory arrest and loss of brain function. The methods used are either:

1. Lethal injection
A lethal injection of Somulose is given into a vein by the vet. The animal may be sedated first and then a catheter is placed into the jugular vein to receive the lethal overdose. The horse should gently collapse to the ground unconscious within thirty seconds and be dead within three minutes. Occasionally there is slight muscle tremor and gasping prior to death. The only disadvantage with this method is disposal of the body, which the vet will advise on. The vet will be responsible for the safety of the handler and decide where to position the horse to perform the injection. The animal's welfare should always come first.

2. Shooting
Any of the above mentioned may shoot the horse using a captive bolt pistol or bell gun. The muzzle of the gun is placed against the animals forehead and fired. The horse falls to the ground immediately. There is usually bleeding from the bullet hole and the nose and paddling movements of the legs. This method is distressing to watch and can be risky for the handler as the horse falls instantly.

Knackermen will destroy horses on the owner's premises or their own and remove the body. They are licensed and listed with the local Authority. They charge more for collecting injected carcases.

Hunt kennelmen have a firearms licence and will destroy horses on their premises or the owner's. They do not accept or collect injected carcases.

Licensed horse slaughtermen shoot horses at the slaughterhouse. The horse must be fit to travel and an appointment has to be made with the slaughterhouse. The carcase is inspected and if passed, a payment will be made according to the carcase weight.

Disposal of the body will depend on local facilities and what method was used to destroy the horse.

The cost of disposal will also vary according to the method chosen.

Cremation

Cremation is available for horses and ponies although it is expensive and the carcase may have to be transported a considerable distance. The Licensed Animal Slaughterers' and Salvage Association (LASSA) provide a nationwide service through their members. Ashes are returned in a casket to the owner.

Incineration

This will be cheaper than cremation but no ashes are returned. Costs vary according to the size of the animal and collection charges.

Burial

The local Environmental Health Department and the National Rivers Authority will advise on the suitability of the burial site. The Ministry of Agriculture, Fisheries and Food (MAFF) limit burial to specific sites away from water courses and drains. The depth of the pit is also specified. The pit has to be dug and machinery available to move the horse's body.

PART FOUR

APPENDICES

NORMAL BLOOD PARAMETERS

HAEMATOLOGY		
Parameter	Normal range	Unit
Red Cell Count	7.8–11	
10^12/L		
Haemoglobin	13–17	g/dl
Packed Cell Volume	0.34–0.46	l/l
White Count	5–12	10^9/L
Neutrophils	2.5–7.5	10^9/L
Lymphocytes	1.5–4.0	10^9/L
Monocytes	<0.5	10^9/L
Eosinophils	<0.5	10^9/L

BIOCHEMISTRY		
Parameter	Normal range	Unit
Total Protein	50–70	g/l
Albumin	25–41	g/l
Globulin	19–36	g/l
Fibrinogen	1–4	g/l
Urea	3.3–7.4	mmol/l
Creatinine	20–177	umol/l
ALT (SGPT)	5–50	IU/L
Alk Phos (ALP)	50–270	IU/L
Gamma GT (GGT)	10–45	IU/L
T. Bilirubin	9–50	umol/l
Bile Acid (fasting)	<10	umol/l
Glucose	3.3–5.8	mmol/l
AST (SGOT)	100–370	IU/L
CK (CPK)	20–225	IU/L
LDH (LD-L)	80–650	IU/L
Sodium	132–146	mmol/l
Potassium	3.3–5.4	mmol/l
Chloride	89–108	mmol/l
Calcium	2.5–3.6	mmol/l
I. Phosphorous	0.9–1.8	mmol/l
Magnesium	0.6–1.0	mmol/l
Cholesterol	2.0–3.6	mmol/l

GLOSSARY OF VETERINARY TERMS

Abdominocentesis The withdrawal of fluid from the abdominal cavity through a needle. Sample used for laboratory tests, especially in colic cases.

Abortion The loss of a foetus under 300 days' gestation.

Abrasion A superficial injury to the skin surface. *See wounds.*

Abscess A cavity containing dead cells, bacteria and inflammatory fluid, i.e. pus. Can occur anywhere in the body. The commonest site is the foot.

Acupuncture A traditional oriental form of healing using fine needles to stimulate specific points or meridians.

Acute The nature of a disease with a sudden, severe onset and a short duration.

Adhesions Fibrous attachments between structures as a result of injury.

Adjuvant A substance added to vaccines to improve their efficacy.

Aerobe A micro-organism that grows in the presence of oxygen.

Afterbirth The foetal membranes that surround the foal in the uterus, which should be expelled within two hours of foaling.

Allergy A hypersensitive reaction to contact with an allergen, e.g. rash or weals due to a local reaction, or inhaled allergens causing constriction of the airways · in COPD.

Alopecia Loss of hair.

Anaemia A condition where there is a reduction in the number of red blood cells or the size of the cells, or a reduction in haemoglobin. This may be caused by an increase in blood loss or cell breakdown, or a decrease in new cell formation.

Anaerobe A micro-organism that lives and grows in the absence of oxygen.

Anaesthetic Either general, where lack of consciousness prevents pain, or local, where the anaesthetic is injected into the skin or around sensory nerves to abolish pain in a localised area.

Analgesia Pain relief. Analgesics are substances that give pain relief, e.g. phenylbutazone.

Aneurysm A bulging of the wall of an artery causing a weakness, e.g. damage to the mesenteric artery in the gut by migrating large redworm larvae.

Anorexia Total lack of appetite.

Anoxia Absence of oxygen.

Antacid A medicine used to correct gut acidity.

Anthelmintic Substances used to treat worm infestation.

Antibiotic Substances that kill (bacteriocidal) or prevent the growth of bacteria (bacteriostatic).

Antibody A part of the immune system that combines with specific antigens to protect the animal against disease.

Antigen A foreign substance to which the body reacts by producing antibodies.

Anti-inflammatory A substance that reduces inflammation.

Antipyretic A substance that reduces body temperature.

Antiseptic A substance that inhibits the growth of micro-organisms and therefore prevents tissue damage.

Antiserum Serum that contains antibodies against specific disease antigens.

Antispasmodic Substances that control overactive gut motility.

Artery Blood vessel that takes oxygen enriched blood from the heart to the rest of the body tissues.

Arthritis Inflammation of a joint which may involve any of the structures around the joint.

Ascarid Intestinal roundworm, seen in horses under two years of age.

Ascites Excessive amounts of abdominal fluid caused by a variety of diseases.

Asepsis Free from sepsis, infective material and bacteria.

Aspiration pneumonia Lung infection caused by inhaling fluid or food into the lungs. May also be caused by drenching with medicines.

Ataxia Inco-ordination of limbs.

Atrophy Wasting or decrease in size of tissues, often due to lack of use.

Auscultate Listen to body sounds, e.g. heart, lungs and guts.

Azoturia. See *exertional myopathy*, equine rhabdomyolysis syndrome.

Bacillus A rod-shaped bacterium, e.g. anthrax, E. coli, tetanus.

Back racking Manually removing faeces from the rectum.

Bacteria Single-celled organisms classified by their shape, size, and reaction to stains and production of spores.

Bilateral Affecting both sides.

Bile Fluid secreted by the liver and passed via the bile duct into the small intestine where it aids fat digestion.

Biopsy A small sample of tissue removed for analysis in the laboratory.

Blepharospasm Spasm of the eyelid muscles in eye disease.

Bog spavin Distension of the tibiotarsal joint (hock) with an excess of synovial fluid.

Bolus A portion of food which has been chewed, mixed with saliva and swallowed.

Borborygmus The sound of food, gas and liquids as they are moved along the alimentary tract by peritalsis.

Bot A fly that lays eggs on the horse's coat, which develop into larvae and pupae in the stomach.

Botulism A fatal paralysing disease caused by toxins from Clostridium botulinum. Seen in equines fed on contaminated big-bale silage.

Bowed tendon Swollen flexor tendons due to inflammation of the tendon and the tendon sheaths.

Bradycardia Slow heart-rate.

Bracken poisoning Bracken contains an enzyme that destroys thiamine and causes inco-ordination, staggering and muscle tremors. It is also carcinogenic and should be removed from horse pasture and destroyed.

Broad-spectrum Having a wide range of activity especially antibiotics that affect a variety of bacteria.

Broken wind Layman's term used to describe emphysema or COPD.

Bruise Bleeding under the skin or sole caused by trauma.

Bursitis Inflammation of a bursal sac, e.g. point of the elbow or hock.

Cachexia Wasting disease or malnutrition.

Callus The formation of new bone at the site of injury e.g. fracture. Palpable as a hard swelling.

Capillaries Small blood-vessels that form a network between the arterioles and venules. They allow the exchange of gases, nutrients and waste products between the blood and the tissues through their thin walls.

Castration An operation to remove the testes performed under general or local anaesthesia.

Catheter A flexible plastic or nylon tube used to administer fluid to and drain fluid from a part of the body, e.g. lacrimal catheter, urinary catheter.

Cellulitis Inflammation and swelling of the subcutaneous tissue due to infection or injury.

Chiropractic Treatment by manipulation of the spine.

Cirrhosis Fibrosis of damaged liver tissue. Seen in ragwort poisoning.

Colostrum A thick milk produced by the mammary glands at foaling containing maternal derived antibodies to protect the foal.

Coprophagia Eating faeces. Seen in adult animals deprived of an adequate diet. Normal behaviour in young foals.

Congenital deformities Those existing at birth, e.g. cleft palate, club foot, over and under shot jaw.

Contagious A disease that is spread from one animal to another.

Contraindicated Drugs that are not advised to be used in certain patients or in conjunction with other medicines. Usually listed on all data sheets.

Crepitus Noise made by fractured ends of bones rubbing together.

Cryosurgery Cold therapy, e.g. liquid nitrogen used to freeze tumour tissue.

Culture Growth of cells on a medium in an incubator at the laboratory, e.g. bacteria and fungi.

Cyanosis Bluish tinge to the mucous membranes caused by lack of oxygen seen in severe respiratory and heart disease.

Cystitis Inflammation of the urinary bladder.

Cytology Examination of cells.

Debride Removal of dead and dying tissue, usually by surgery.

Dehydration Condition caused by loss of body water.

Dermatitis Inflammation of the skin.

Desmitis Inflammation of ligament.

Diagnose To identify a disease or condition.

Disinfectant Substance used to kill bacteria on inanimate objects, not to be used on living tissue.

Dysphagia Difficulty in swallowing.

Ectoparasites Parasites that live on the body surface, e.g. ticks, lice, mites.

Electrolytes Salts found in body fluids necessary for various functions, e.g. conducting nerve impulses and muscle contraction.

Embolism A blood clot or foreign material that blocks a blood-vessel.

Endoparasites Parasites found inside the body, e.g. lungworm, redworm.

Endorphins Chemicals released from the brain that relieve pain and produce a sense of well-being.

Endoscope A surgical instrument used to visualise internal organs by fibre optics inside a thin, flexible tube.

Epistaxis Nose bleed.

Exudate A mixture of inflammatory cells and fluid that have leaked from blood vessels into tissue or onto the surface of tissues.

Fascia Sheets of fibrous tissue found between muscle layers.

Febrile High temperature or fever.

Fluke A parasite of the liver found in sheep, cattle and equines.

Fungicide A substance used to kill fungi.

Gelding A castrated male horse.

Gingivitis Inflammation of the gums.

Glossitis Inflammation of the tongue.

Gonitis Inflammation of the stifle joint.

Haematology The study of blood cells.

Haemoglobin The oxygen carrying pigment of red blood cells that contain iron.

Haemostasis   The stopping of haemorrhage.

Hepatitis   Inflammation of the liver.

Hereditary   Genetically passed on to the next generation, as in hereditary diseases, e.g. Immunodeficiency disease in Arab foals, umbilical hernias.

Hernia   A condition where an organ or tissue protrudes through a break in the enclosing muscular wall. May be hereditary or a result of injury.

Histology   The study of the structure of tissues.

Hormone   A chemical produced by a specific gland in the body that regulates the activity of target tissue.

Hygroma   The swelling of a bursa with an excess of synovial fluid due to trauma, e.g. seen on the carpus.

Hyperlipaemia   A serious, often fatal condition where the body fat is mobilised into the blood. Common in small ponies and donkeys on starvation diets.

Hypersensitivity   The overreaction of the body to a foreign substance.

Icterus   Yellow discolouration of the skin, mucous membranes and organs, i.e. jaundice.

Ileus   Lack of intestinal movement (peristalsis).

Immunity   Resistance to infection. May be natural or acquired.

Incubation   The time between contact with a disease and exhibiting the clinical signs of that disease.

Infection   A condition caused by micro-organisms.

Infra-red thermography   A technique used to detect areas of injury/inflammation by mapping temperature differences in the tissues due to the alteration in blood flow and cell activity.

Insecticide   A substance that kills insects.

Intussusception   The telescoping of a piece of intestine into the adjoining segment causing a blockage of the gut lumen. This requires surgical intervention.

Ischaemia   Lack of blood supply to an area resulting in cell death.

Jugular refill test   A indicator of the status of the circulatory system. The jugular vein is emptied by thumb pressure down the jugular groove and the time taken to refill while pressure is maintained is measured in seconds.

Keratitis   Inflammation of the cornea of the eye.

Knee   The carpus joint of the horse.

Lateral   On the outside cf. *medial* on the inside.

Lavage   Flush out with fluid.

Lymphangitis   Inflammation of the lymphatic vessels and lymph nodes.

Lysis   Destruction of cells.

Malnutrition   Incorrect feeding or diet.

Metabolism   Chemical activity in cells which provides energy for bodily functions.

Metastasis   Spread of neoplasms within the body from one part to another, usually via the blood or lymphatic system.

Mucopurulent   A mixture of mucus and pus.

Mucous membrane   The lining epithelial cells of all hollow organs, e.g. digestive, urogenital and respiratory system.

Myopathy   Muscle disease.

Myositis   Inflammation of muscle.

Necrosis   Death of cells by disease.

Neoplasm   An abnormal growth or tumour.

Neurectomy   Surgically cutting a nerve.

Obesity   Excessively overweight, a serious welfare problem in western society.

Oedema   Accumulation of fluid in the tissues outside the cells, e.g. filled legs, ventral oedema, ascites.

Ossify   To develop into bone.

Osteitis   Inflammation of bone.

Pathogen   A micro-organism that causes disease.

Peristalsis   Muscular contractions that propel food along the digestive tract.

Polydipsia   Excessive thirst and drinking.

Polyuria   Passing excessive volumes of urine.

Prophylaxis   Preventive treatment, e.g. vaccines.

Pruritus   Itching and scratching.

Pyrexia   High temperatures or fever.

Quarantine   Isolation to prevent spread of disease.

Quidding   Dropping chewed food from the mouth.

Radiograph   An X-ray plate or film.

Rhinitis   Inflammation of the nasal mucosa.

Rig   A male horse with an undescended testicle in the abdomen or inguinal canal.

Roaring   An abnormal inspiratory noise.

Sedative   A substance that acts on the central nervous system and reduces the level of awareness.

Septicaemia   Presence of pathogens and their toxins in the blood.

Sequestrum   A fragment of bone that has lost its blood supply – caused by injury or infection. Requires surgical intervention.

Sinusitis   Inflammation of the sinuses.

Subcutaneous   Under the skin.

Tranquilliser   A substance that has a calming effect without producing sedation.

Topical   A local area, as in topical application of cream.

Urticaria   An allergic skin reaction.

Vice   Stereotypical behaviour, e.g. crib biting, weaving.

Suggested Further Reading

B.H.S. Welfare leaflets on health care/general management.

B.H.S. Road Safety Leaflet.

Colour Atlas of Diseases and Disorders of the Horse. Knottenbelt and Pascoe: Mosby Wolfe. ISBN 0 7234 1 702 4.

Current Therapy in Equine Medicine. 4th edn. Robinson: W.B. Saunders.

Equine Injury, Therapy and Rehabilitation. 2nd edn. Bromily: Blackwell Science.

Explaining Laminitis and its prevention. (1992) Robert A. Eustace: E.F.S. equine series ISBN 0 95189 740 3.

Farewell, making the right decision. Published by Humane Slaughter Association. ISBN 1 87156 106 X.

Feeding and Watering. Teresa Hollands: Crowood Press ISBN 1 85223 809 7

Horse Owner's Guide to Lameness. Stashak: Williams and Wilkinson Publication. ISBN 0 68307 985 9.

Poisonous Plants in Britain and their effects on Animals and Man. (1984) M.R. Cooper and A.W. Johnson: MAFF London Ref Book 161.

Veterinary Notes for Horse Owners, Revised. (1996) Peter Rossdale: Ebury Press. ISBN 0 09171 511 3.

Useful Addresses

Association of Chartered Physiotherapists in Animal
    Therapy
Moorland House
Salters Lane
Winchester
Hants
SO22 5JP

Tel 01962 863801

British Association of Homeopathic Veterinary
    Surgeons
Chinham House
Stanford in the Vale
Nr Faringdon
Oxfordshire
SN7 8NQ

Tel 01367 710324

British Equine Veterinary Association
Administration Secretary
5 Findlay Street
London
SW6 6HE

Tel 0171 610 6080

British Horse Society
Stoneleigh Deer Park
Kenilworth
Warwickshire
CV8 2XZ

Tel 01926 707700

Farriers' Registration Council
Sefton House
Adam Court
Newark Road
Peterborough
PE1 5PP

Tel 01733 319911

Laminitis Clinic
Mead House Farm
Dauntsey
Chippenham
Wiltshire
SN15 4JA

Tel 01249 890784

Licensed Animal Slaughterers' and Salvage
    Association (LASSA)
Birch House
Birch Vale
Stockport
Cheshire
SK12 5DH

Tel 01663 744154

Ministry of Agriculture, Fisheries and Food (MAFF)
Hook Rise South
Tolworth
Surbiton
Surrey
KT6 7DX

Tel 0181 3304411

Royal College of Veterinary Surgeons
Belgravia House
62–64 Horse Ferry Road
London SW1P 2AF

Tel 0171 222 2001

Society of Master Saddlers
Kettles Farm
Mickfield
Stowmarket
Suffolk

Tel 01499 711642

INDEX